Moments of Truth

Centre for
Faith and Spirituality
Loughborough University

Moments of Truth

edited by
Tony Jasper

Marshall Pickering

Marshall Morgan and Scott
Marshall Pickering
34–42 Cleveland Street, London, W1P 5FB, UK.

First published in 1990 by Marshall Morgan and Scott
Publications Ltd
Part of the Marshall Pickering Holdings Group

British Library Cataloguing in Publication Data

Jasper, Tony
  Moments of truth.
  1. Christian life – personal observations
  I. Title
  248.4

ISBN 0 551 01876 3

Text set in 10/12 pt Palacio by Avocet Robinson, Buckingham
Printed in Great Britain by Cox & Wyman Ltd, Reading

To Helen Morton, Jenny Cook, Erica Schmidt and Bonny Dobson.

Thanks to Cathryn Tanner, my editor at Marshalls, for endless patience.

Contents

ACKNOWLEDGMENTS

Extracts from *On The Side of The Angels* by John Smith, and *The Everyday Book* by Mary Batchelor (Sheila Cassidy extract), are reproduced by kind permission of Lion Publishing.

The extracts from *God Put A Fighter In Me* by Sheila Walsh and *Power Evangelism* by John Wimber with Kevin Spring are reproduced by kind permission of Hodder & Stoughton.

Extracts from *Steps Of Faith* (Geoffrey and Judith Stevenson) © 1984, and *Worship* by Graham Kendrick © 1984 are reproduced by kind permission of Kingsway Publications Ltd, 1 St Anne's Road, Eastbourne, East Sussex.

Adapted extracts: Adrian Plass and Mary Whitehouse, by very kind permission of *21st Century Christian*, and of the subjects concerned.

Paul Davis is thanked for adaptation of material about Marilyn Baker and Cliff Barrows that appeared in *New Christian Media*.

INTRODUCTION

This book is not primarily intended to be read straight through from cover to cover. It is a book for quieter moments, reflective times, and hopefully will offer inspiration, especially when things seem pointless. I cannot say I go along with some of the things said in this book, even though I put it together and certainly asked for the contributions. But so be it! It's never easy accepting that other people perceive and think differently or have walked the inner journey of life in ways that puzzle an outsider but mean much to them. I would expect some puzzlement from you, as well, even if you dip into the text at random. However, let another human 'be': cease bringing your own luggage, and expect to receive. Respect another, learn from another, and take it as a privilege that someone lets you into their unique world, albeit just a little of it. Sometimes during the text I wept, at other moments laughed, but in each there is inherent the thought that 'the best that can happen to anyone, or to the world, is to be filled with all the fullness of God'[1] – to be part of His purpose.

God never leaves us for one moment without reason to praise him. Even if we were to find ourselves with no prayers apparently answered, no good things to enjoy and give thanks for, the joys of life stolen away from us, yet his unchanging character, his faithfulness and love would still provide good enough reasons to give him the best our hearts can offer. His command is an invitation, his invitation affords us

[1] *The Use of Praying*, J. Neville Ward (Epworth, 1967), p. 90.

entrance into his presence, and in his presence we find an infinite number of good reasons to praise him. As David asserts in Psalm 16.11, 'You will fill me with joy in your presence, with eternal pleasures at your right hand'.

Graham Kendrick, *Worship* (Kingsway).

The Bible frequently points us toward experiences that we have not already had, implying that as we have these experiences we will grow in biblical knowledge. Sacrificial love of Christian brothers and sisters and acts of mercy are like that; as we obey, light reflects from our good works back on Scripture, revealing more about God's grace and mercy. So God uses our experiences to show us more fully what he teaches in Scripture, many times toppling or altering elements of our theology and worldviews. That is what he accomplished with the disciples through their experience of his crucifixion and resurrection. Only then were they able to understand his earlier words at the temple to the Jews: 'Destroy this temple, and I will raise it again in three days.'

John Wimber, *Power Evangelism*
(Hodder and Stoughton)

NINOY AQUINO

Ninoy was born on 27th November, 1932, in the Tarlac Province of the Philippines. He was exceptionally gifted and after a series of major jobs he was seen by many as successor to President Marcos. When Marcos imposed martial law in 1972 Ninoy was arrested. During his imprisonment he became convinced that Jesus was indeed the Way, the Truth, the Life.

Ninoy Aquino worked initially in journalism, and then when sent with a detachment of Philippine soldiers to take part in the Korean War he covered himself in glory, so that he was later awarded the Philippine Legion of Honour. He became the *Manila Times* foreign correspondent for South-east Asia. Later he studied law and became a special assistant to President Ramon Magsaysay. In 1954 he married Corazon (Cory) Cojuanco, a member of one of the most wealthy and prominent families. Many further honours came his way, so much so that he was increasingly recognised as a successor to Marcos. He was among the first arrested when martial law was declared in 1972. He was charged with murder and subversion and sentenced to death, but international protest saw a commutation of his sentence to life imprisonment. During his prison stay he was put on a starvation diet for several months in solitary confinement.

While in this situation he wrote these words to a friend:

In the loneliness of my solitary confinement in Laur, in the depths of my solitude and desolation, during those long hours of meditation, I found my inner peace. God stood me face-to-face with myself and forced me to look at my emptiness and nothingness, and then helped me to discover Him who has never really left my side. But because pride shielded my eyes, and the lust for earthly and temporal power, honour and joys drugged my mind, I failed to notice Him.

I prayed and meditated on the life of Jesus from birth to the Ascension. Suddenly Jesus became a live human being. His life was to become my inspiration. Here was a God-Man who preached nothing but love and was rewarded with death. Here was a God-Man who had power over all creation, but took all the mockery of a crown of thorns with humility and patience. And for all these noble intentions, He was shamed, vilified, slandered and betrayed.

Then it dawned on me how puny were my sufferings compared to His whose only purpose was to save Mankind from eternal damnation.

With that realisation, I went down on my knees and begged forgiveness. I knew I was merely undergoing a test, maybe in preparation for another mission. I knew everything that happens in this world is with His knowledge and consent. I therefore resigned myself to His will.

'Thy will be done!' These words snatched me from the jaws of death. In Laur, I gave up my life and offered it to Him, picked up my cross and followed Him.

MARILYN BAKER

Marilyn Baker studied piano and oboe at the Royal College
of Music, London. Overcoming her blindness, she became
a very talented singer-songwriter-musician and enjoys
considerable popularity for her ability to communicate faith
and enjoyment. Apart from having had a number of major
selling albums in the Christian world, she is much wanted
as a live performer.

For Marilyn Baker each day is taken as it comes. 'I
don't tend to look too far ahead. Every day, I seek
strength for that day. It sounds ever so spiritual to say
that but my biggest hope is that I'll be doing what God
really wants me to do and that I'll remain in the centre
of His will.'

She speaks of people coming to her saying that her
music has been such a blessing. 'At one point I came
to the stage where I thought "If Christ suddenly took
it all away, would I still be able to be really fulfilled
as a Christian?" I think I can honestly say that I believe
He has called me into this work for this moment in
time. I am involved in it, not because it's the be-all and
end-all, but because He is the one I love. My greatest
aim is to be doing what He wants and to keep Him
in the centre of what I'm doing. Then I know I'll be
really fulfilled. I might have a lot of success as far as
record sales go, but that is just a by-product.'

When she views her life it is to see her role as
someone sowing the seed and opening people's minds
to what the possibilities are. And she readily admits,
'We all get ups and downs on the way in our lives . . .
I personally have been through a lot. It's been hard

for me to keep on the road at times.'

And aside from her musical ministry she has fought to see that handicapped people in churches feel accepted. 'They can give each other something. Before I became a reasonably well-known singer I used to find it very hard to find my niche in churches. People who are handicapped are usually on the receiving end of things. But it's lovely for them to be able to give. If people want to know how they can show love to people who are handicapped in any way, one of the most lovely things they can do is to get to know them as an individual, and invite them into their homes. It may be difficult for them to begin with, not quite knowing how to deal with people. I found one of the hardest things to cope with was the sense of not feeling accepted as a natural person.'

For a special moment of truth we can travel back to her early years, to experiences at a lively evangelical Anglican church and a Brethren Assembly – it was through the latter that she was baptised when eighteen years of age. 'At that time I was studying for my A level exam in Scripture. My teacher was very liberal and she was knocking all the things I had based my faith on. Although you are supposed to study these things without letting them affect you, I found I couldn't! It was really affecting me. Every time I took my doubts to my friends, they would really helpfully sort them out for me. They were my spiritual parents.'

Later when she went to the Royal College of Music she felt herself growing as a Christian. 'The Christian Union actually went to the trouble of printing their programme in Braille and sending it to me. (They didn't know me, so they didn't know whether I was a Christian or not.) They told me: ''We have prayer meetings and they last for an hour.'' I thought,

''Prayer meetings, for an hour?'' But I went along. My Christian friends stuck very close to me. They helped me with my lessons and lectures and they really did support me in every way. They showed their Christianity by loving me. Spiritually many of them were a lot more advanced than I was. So I learned a lot from them. It was one of the richest periods of Christian fellowship in my life.' Moments of truth.

CLIFF BARROWS

~

For countless millions of Christians no Billy Graham broadcast or campaign meeting seems valid without the presence of Cliff Barrows! He has been choir leader with the Evangelistic Team since 1948.

For Cliff Barrows it's almost an impossibility that someone can be a Christian and yet not wish to express the praise of God in music. For him it's been a lifetime in which he has expressed what God means to him in melody, although technically he's never received a training that might be described as befitting a highly professional phase of music. He did study various forms of music and harmony but wistfully says, 'I wish I could play the piano . . . I wish I could do a lot of things!' He claims, 'I entered Christian music work because I felt God was calling me.' And so Cliff Barrows has become part and parcel of all Billy Graham campaign meetings in which he has shown his calling to lead music and encourage people to sing. 'Like all people in the Billy Graham team I have been surprised and humbled that God has chosen and used such human vessels as ourselves to glorify His Name. Whatever place God calls us to, whether it's to a large or small work, it's a great privilege.' For Cliff, it's a case of 'learning to be available to God where we are. In doing God's will – whatever it is – there is fulfilment. It is certainly true in my experience.'

His work with Billy Graham has meant long periods away from home and he can remember one of his sons praying when he was eight years old, 'Dear Jesus, please save everyone in the world so Daddy can stay at home.' Along the way Cliff has found excitement, challenge, joy – and yes, many moments of truth. His association with Dr Graham goes back to 1948 and he remembers then a precious moment of truth, when he realised that here, with this evangelist, he would find his life's work. 'I said to Mr Graham that for however long my wife and I were wanted in the work we would be willing. I have never doubted once that this situation is where God wanted me to be. Opportunities may have come, perhaps to settle down and go into a church, but I've never been tempted by it. God has given me that desire to follow through on this course. I believe that's the reason we've been together for so long. Not many organisations can claim to have a group of people who started it and have been together for forty years. It has been God who has kept us on the target for His will and purpose.'

Cliff Barrows has had mixed fortunes in health over the past years, but there he was once more in 1989 with Billy Graham and George Beverly Shea saying and singing 'This is my story, this is my song'.

MARY BATCHELOR

❦

Mary is a freelance writer and conference speaker. For a number of years she taught both English and Religious Education. She is the author of several books, and has edited some highly successful compilations including The Lion Book Of Children's Prayers *and its companion volume,* **The Lion Book of Bible Stories and Prayers**.

I climbed out of bed, knelt down and prayed. It was better, I decided, to be safe than sorry. I suppose I was five or six at the time and had already listened to a good number of sermons, some fiery, some persuasive, telling me of the need to repent and give my heart to Jesus. Each time the appeal came my doubts returned. So I repeated the required response, just in case it hadn't worked last time.

Perhaps I am unduly cynical. God, in his mercy, may well have come into my life on that first remembered occasion. But I *do* regret the anxiety and the guilty feelings that lingered. God, I felt sure, was Someone who found me a constant disappointment and for whom I rarely came up to the mark. I could scarcely expect much love from him or feel much in return.

I was certainly influenced by the hard and fast thinking of some evangelicals of the time but also — thank God — by the real and generous Christian faith of both my parents.

God came in at the back door instead of the front. I began by knowing God, and the way of salvation, in my head. The heart has followed. I no longer regret the absence of a blinding moment of truth but relish the way in which, as I grow older, I become more and more aware of the warmth and sufficiency of God's love. Now I can believe, with joy, that I am accepted in Christ. I can set my feelings free to enjoy God in response.

Much of the time, the truth of God's love and involvement with me has still to be accepted by faith rather than feelings. Like C.S. Lewis, I am thankful when I am 'surprised by joy' and his presence becomes overwhelmingly real.

One such moment came when our second child was born. The birth of our first child had been particularly difficult and I was feeling very frightened. I went into labour at home on a bright Monday morning in late November. The midwife and I waited for the doctor to arrive. My husband – last source of comfort – had been banished from the room. Suddenly a sense of utter well-being and comfort flooded through me. The knowledge that God was with me was more real than the pain or the familiar surroundings of my own bedroom. When the doctor arrived he looked at me in surprise and said, 'You look so peaceful and relaxed – not even pethidine can do that!'

'The road the righteous travel is like the sunrise, getting brighter and brighter until daylight has come' (Prov. 4.18). That seems to me to be a good way to experience Christian living. I hope and pray that the light does grow stronger to the end of the journey, when we reach the city that has no need of the sun, 'because the glory of God shines on it and the Lamb is its lamp'.

NICK BEGGS

Nick Beggs found fame with the pop group Kajagoogoo. After that group's demise he founded the short-lived Kaja. He became part of Ellis, Beggs & Howard, a trio that found pop fortune at the end of the eighties.

Nick Beggs was born on 15th December, 1961. He was born with blue eyes and his hair was probably brown. In pop times his mop has even been described as a 'peroxide explosion with beads' while fans have affectionately called him 'fluffy chicken'.

His parents separated when he was ten and he stayed with his mother and sister Jacqueline. He remembers his dad gave him a drum kit and when he was around fifteen he began learning acoustic guitar. School was a bore and when he left he decided to do something he enjoyed. Music was the best option.

However, he was sensible enough to take a foundation course in art and design; but his art school years were marred by tragedy at home. 'My mother had cancer, and had, in fact, kept it quiet. I had the painful experience of watching her waste away.' Her illness and death shook him to the core and stretched him almost beyond endurance. He was seventeen when she died. 'Technically because of her age Jacqueline should have been taken into local authority care, and I had to prove to the authorities I was responsible enough to be the head of the family.'

He coped, just. He began to ask a great many religious questions. Obviously he could have denounced the Christian God, but he did not; he just thought religious faith was an irrelevance. Drugs took him away from reality and he was involved in various casual relationships. He used people and lost many friends.

But a great change in his life and overall perceptions lay ahead. He met a keen Christian by the name of Ken, who told him some of the basic things on which living faith rests. Nick realised he was in great need of forgiveness and yet, he says, 'I realised I couldn't expect it from people I'd hurt, however much I said I was sorry. I wanted to wipe the slate clean and start again.'

Nick learnt about Jesus, especially why he died and how through his death God could be found responsive and longing to forgive. So there came the precious moment when Nick's moment of truth dawned – 'God's son had died for me' and 'I claimed this love.'

Since then life has had its 'ups and downs' but Nick's precious moment remains to underpin the normal anxieties and trials of life. 'Everything I do now in music I do through faith. I feel that God needs to fill me up so that I'm doing what He wants.' In musical terms, in the face of much negativeness that pervades a great many pop lyrics, he says, 'I want to give people another option – I mean all is relative, all insignificant when considered in terms of eternity.'

JOHNNY CASH

Johnny Cash was born on 26th February, 1932, in Kingsland, Arkansas, one of seven children born to Ray and Carrie Cash. He has been a recording star for over thirty years with around 500 albums catalogued. He was the youngest man ever selected for the prestigious American Country Music Hall of Fame. He has won countless Grammy Awards, has had countless hit records and received at least twenty-three BMI Awards for songwriting. Cash is more than a country star, more than a pop influence. His music and life have in so many ways epitomised both the music and spirit of the American people.

Interviewed shortly before his visit to Britain under the title of The Johnny Cash Route '89 Tour, the American country rock singer of almost legendary status commented, 'I'm someone who has got that wild streak, that black dog inside of me, that wants to bite. But now I feel great, better than ever.'

In the early sixties, Cash looked for happiness through drugs and, finding little satisfaction, he contemplated suicide. It had all begun in seeming innocence; like many he took a few stimulants to ease tiredness and then some tranquillisers for relaxation. Whereas many people go no further, for Cash it was the beginning of a journey that almost ended in his disintegration. It all reached its climax in the now much recounted tale of how a policeman found him slumped, listless and aimless and transported him to the police station so that he could sleep off the effects of drug taking. Cash says, 'I woke up in jail and I didn't remember how I got there!'

During this period he began to gain a bad reputation in the club circuit for being unreliable and people knew this strong, big-built man wasn't entirely his own master. It was sad to say, but sentiment and affection could not hide the ugly reality that here was a powerful human being with endless potential who was intent on self-destruction.

It seems a trifle easy to say that for Cash the 'new way' of self-understanding and living was commitment to the Christian faith of two thousand years, but it was so. It was a simple trust in Jesus that became his new life, once his moment of truth dawned – the truth that he was wasting the mind, body and especially the voice that he had been given by the Creator. And although there have been some difficult times he has stayed there with Jesus, so that at the end of the eighties, Adam Sweeting, a major British music writer, could say, 'God fills the gap where there used to be drug addiction and a suicidal streak.'

The 'new' Cash, the continuing in faith Cash, owed much to the American evangelist Billy Graham. 'He's been a good friend of mine and has prayed for me a lot.' After his first marriage collapsed, he married June Carter from the famous American 'country' family. June was the youngest daughter of Mother Maybelle Carter. Cash had moved into a deeply religious family where people walked in their Saviour's footsteps and this too made a major difference in his life. Cash had always been religious but had never found personal faith, and with his turning from the darkness of drugs he was to say, 'I've seen the Light! I've always been a deeply religious person but these days the light's shining a little brighter!' Pat Boone's wife Shirley comments, 'He has been filled with the Holy Spirit, as has his wife June.'

Cash sang of the people who work and sweat for the American dream, long before the advent of more recent American troubadours like Bob Seger, Bruce Springsteen and John Cougar Mellenchamp. And his Christian underpinning has led him to perform dozens of prison concerts, to spearhead drives for prison reform, correspond with countless prisoners and aid many of them to return to society. So, too, he has championed the cause of the American Red Indian. He has supported mental health associations, homes for autistic children, refuges for battered women, the American Cancer Society, YWCA, Youth for Christ and Campus Life.

All his many works owe their existence to the one moment of truth when he was confronted with the claims of his own life and made intensely aware of the victory won for him by Jesus Christ.

SHEILA CASSIDY

Sheila Cassidy trained as a doctor, went to Chile to escape the academic rat race and became closely involved in treating the poor and forgotten. Following an extreme right-wing coup, she treated a wounded guerrilla soldier and was arrested. After torture and imprisonment, she was expelled from the country. While in prison she established workshops to utilise every precious scrap of material. She shared her faith with many who had grown up to hate the Church, but who desired to know her strength under torture. She now works as the Medical Director of St Luke's Hospice in Plymouth.

The car threaded its way slowly through the streets of Santiago, crossing and re-crossing the same network of streets and houses.

'Which street? Which house?'

The questions were repeated continuously, and Sheila Cassidy, sitting beside the man with the gun in the front of car, could not answer.

When she was arrested, Sheila thought that a phone-call to the British Embassy would soon solve her problem. Instead, she was taken into a small bare room, told to strip naked, then, blindfolded and gagged, she was strapped to a metal bed. The electric current was switched on and the questions began. At each question, an electric shock passed through her body, strengthening in intensity until she answered. Determined not to betray the nuns who had sheltered the wounded guerrilla, Sheila invented the area, street and house where she treated his wounds.

Now they were driving her there to verify the details

she had given. At any moment they would guess she had been lying. One of the men said, 'It would be easier to kill her now.' She sat still, realising she would probably die.

Suddenly, God seemed very far away and unreal. Had belief in him all been a fairy story? Then, after a moment, with no rush of emotion or feeling of exhaltation, Sheila suddenly knew with absolute certainty that God *did* exist. She stretched out a hand of faith to the God, who seemed so far away, but was *real*.

GERALD COATES

～

*Gerald Coates is one of the best known names and faces in the New Church and House Church movement. He witnesses powerfully to the blessing of the Holy Spirit. Among the new movement he has arguably been **the** instigator of much sharing with mainstream Evangelical Christians. He is author of a number of books including **Divided We Stand**.*

I was just nineteen and I had a fairly good job in the West End. I was the youngest display manager in the United Kingdom.

Also I had had an experience of the Holy Spirit. Some people used to gather in our home to pray, to learn about growing together, seeking the Lord's will. I was questioning what I ought to be doing with my life.

I decided I should leave my well paid job. Eighteen months later all our savings were gone and I was either too spiritual or too proud to share our predicament with friends. We really did get to a point as a family when we had no money. The only thing we seemed to have was sugar! There was nothing in the bank, nothing to translate into ready cash.

I remember one particular day when the milkman called. My wife was in tears when he came up the path, as we had nothing to pay him. We heard him come and go. Perhaps it was something to do with a strict Brethren background, but my wife could not resist opening the door, calling after him and asking about the due payment.

The milkman said it was all paid. Someone near us had paid the bill and they had also paid for a big bag of goods that we suddenly noticed next to the milk on the doorstep.

We just cried, that this should happen, that it should happen to us, on that very day, the day when we so badly needed such gifts. It meant so much to us. We knew God saw our predicament and supplied our needs. This was a moment of truth for us. I think we had belonged to those who talk of God's goodness, who had heard of God's goodness but either never believed it could be for us or had not seen it for ourselves. This was a time of truth for us. Suddenly we knew the Lord would protect us. Doubtless we had not lifted our hearts to Him, for He is gracious.

I think many a time God catches us off our guard. Things so to speak done behind our back! Since then I've learnt so much, seen so much more of God at work and spoken about His graciousness.

WENDY CRAIG

Wendy Craig is one of Britain's most favoured and popular actresses, both in television and the theatre. She is married and lives amidst beautiful countryside, in rural Berkshire.

When I was a little girl I felt very much part of God's family. I felt close to God and loved to say my prayers and I knew He was my father in heaven. I really trusted and believed. As I grew older I began to feel I didn't need Him, that I could live my life my own way, so I drifted away from Him but the Good Shepherd that He is, He had his crook around me and brought me back to the fold.

'In worldly terms I did well and had a fairly successful existence, but gradually as I grew older I realised there was something missing from my life. There was an emptiness. I suppose my soul was empty and I knew that the relationship I had with God as a child was something I must rediscover. I had a big and beautiful dog called Tallis, an English setter. Around where I lived there was beautiful countryside and so we went for many a walk. I remember one night after I had gone to bed I heard him humping around and when I went to see I found him on the stairs. He had been taken ill and had tried to get upstairs, and along the way he had fallen. I realised he was dying, so I cradled him and talked and he just died. I was desperately fond of him and we had spent so much time together. I was sad and my sadness grew into despair. It was then that I suddenly found myself one day wandering into church, and I started praying.

I suppose I realised that in all my walks with Tallis

23

around the countryside I had been communicating with God in a very basic and simple way, thanking him for the peace and joy that I was getting from His creation, the beauty that was surrounding me, the seasons and all their variations and the varied weather, and that we had walked through it all together. After the death of Tallis I had stopped going on these walks. I felt deprived of these wonderful moments with God, so in the church I asked (and I realised that I needed to do so) God to forgive me for thinking I was so clever that I could do everything for myself. I really did feel sorry and I was in need of forgiveness. I felt I needed to be forgiven and that there was a new start to be made.

So this was my moment of conversion, real conversion, when I really became a Christian in the true sense and knew that from that moment I would try and serve the Father in the best way I could, with His help.

MARGARET CUNDIFF

*Margaret Cundiff is a Deacon in the Church of England at St James Church, Selby. She is Broadcasting Officer of the York Diocese and is the Anglican adviser to Yorkshire Television. Her claim to national fame in Britain is her frequent appearances on Radio 2's **Derek Jamieson Show**. She also broadcasts on BFBS.*

I have experienced both truth in the noise and truth in the silence. Being part of a crowd and suddenly, whoosh, being taken out of it, not physically, but mentally and spiritually. God grabbing me by the scruff of my neck and saying 'I want to talk to you *now*, no ifs or buts, *now*!' A friend once said to me, 'Never ignore the nudges of God.' I couldn't ignore them if I tried. They are compelling, and I have been forced to listen, but it has always been 'something to my advantage' – even though it may have been painful.

Then there are the times of silence when God has spoken in the quiet, in the stillness when I have been longing He might, and in that time I have known the presence – the power – of God and that all was in hand, all was well, there was nothing to fear – ever.

In noise and in silence, but also in sound and colour. In North Yorkshire where I live, at the end of harvesting each summer, after the corn, wheat or barley has been gathered in, the stubble is burnt. It's a frightening and awe-inspiring sight. Fields on fire, the smoke swirling and almost leering across. I hated it, because I have a fear of fires, remembering wartime scenes – the red sky, the smell of smoke – and asking my father what it was. 'That's Manchester on fire,' he said. I was scared the fire might run towards us and gobble us up, as I had seen it happen on the newsreel. It didn't, but the memory remains, and so seeing blackened fields, the heat, the destruction in the gentle countryside I love brings back those memories of a destructive evil force so long ago. I talked about my fears to a friend who pointed me to Paul's letter to the Corinthians, chapter three, where he talks about our work being burnt up, the chaff of life, the useless, the false, the showy, all gone in a puff of smoke. That chat did nothing to help me, only make me feel more insecure, and so year by year as I saw the fields burn, I felt only fear and anxiety. I searched my life and saw only stubble, straw and hay.

Then a couple of years ago as the burning time came round again, I stood looking at the scene, felt the fear rising within me, and then I heard an almost audible voice say, 'Margaret, when you walk through the fire you shall not be burned, and the flame shall not consume you. For I am the Lord your God, the Holy One of Israel, your Saviour. You are precious in my eyes, and honoured and I love you.' I knew I'd heard those words before, and it wasn't until I looked them up that I realised they were from the book of Isaiah. I must have heard and read them so many times without them making any impression on me, but here they were coming clearly, just for me, at just that time. It was a joyful moment of truth, a release, and I could look at the burning fields without fear.

I realised in that moment I was free to be happy, to laugh, to enjoy myself, and God, my God, my Father, loved to see me doing so. He wasn't going to hit me over the head for enjoying myself or force me into unnatural solemnity. Laughter, a sense of the ridiculous and the ability to make others laugh were gifts to be used, and not to be consigned to an almighty funeral pyre as worthless, frivilous activities. I was fireproofed by His love! The fire no longer looked threatening but like glittering, sparkling jewels, dancing, leaping for joy.

A couple of weeks later I walked by the fields, stopped and looked. There were appearing bright new blades of grass, springing up, not consumed at all, but free to grow. It was God's gift of new life. It was as if He was saying, 'So why were you afraid?' – and as I looked I began to laugh, and I knew it was all right, and it will be all right, always.

DANA

Dana, alias Rosemary Brown, came to the fore in 1970 when she won the Eurovision Song Contest for Ireland with the song 'All Kinds of Everything'. Since then she has had numerous successful singles and albums and appeared in countless television shows and theatre presentations. Along the way she had a major religious experience that has transformed her life.

There was a moment when I actually became aware that Jesus is real. And it changed my whole concept of God.

I was part of a small gathering, a prayer group, no more than eight people, and quite honestly I found the experience terrifying. I felt terribly threatened. I remember my heart pounding away and I wanted to get out of the situation. I felt it was all alien and I did not belong. These people were praying about their lives and they were saying things about themselves. I thought it was an inexplicable affair. I even thought it faintly ridiculous but I did have a respect for them, since I knew them and they were good people. I was particularly worried by the presence of a nun and a priest and I think my anxiety focused on them. They prayed over me. It seemed terrifying and I knew that what was being said was not going through my ears, but was bypassing my brain. I felt it all to be rather abstract; it was, I suppose, how I felt about God. But I was somehow soaking in what they were saying. I began to feel bubbly and there was an excitement that spread through my body, rising to my face and I wanted to smile and smile. I felt totally loved; it was an overwhelming experience, numbing me in its intensity. It was real love in a way not associated with human and earthly love for and with another. I felt trapped by it. It was amazing, for I hadn't given much to this whole affair. I can't explain it – I felt so complete. I knew that something was reaching to me. I had gone through intellectual argument about God, but this was quite different, for here was God soaking through me, so deep, to the very centre of me.

PAUL DAVIS

❧

*Paul Davis founded and became President of the **Gospel Music Association** (UK), and for over 20 years has been involved in journalism and radio. For over ten years he published and edited **New Christian Music**, later titled **New Christian Music Media**. He has broadcast on a number of radio stations and hosted both gospel and country music series. He is the founder of **New Music Enterprises** which handles the Christian activities and bookings of some well-known Christian artistes.*

My wife, Hazel, and I were married in 1965 and in the happy ensuing years we enjoyed the blessings of Christian marriage and family life. We proved that God blesses those who do their best to honour Him. Our life was further enriched when our home was blessed by the birth of a daughter, Anita, and then by the birth of a son, Wesley. We enjoyed the continual delights of seeing them growing up.

The birth of Anita was a special blessing after the heartache of Hazel suffering two miscarriages and nearly losing Anita in the early months of that pregnancy. Hazel says, 'I can identify very well with other women who have suffered the same disappointment that I felt during those times. I can remember the first time it happened, feeling so bewildered, hurt and, yes, angry with God for first giving me a child and then taking it away again. I have always wanted a family. My great ambition in life was to be simply a wife and mother. And here was God seemingly giving me that dream and then taking it away again. I have always been aware of God's presence with me, even when I was a child. But suddenly it seemed as if the Light had gone out of my life. God no longer seemed near. I tried to pray but seemed to be talking to the ceiling!

'Paul was such a great help then. He kept quoting to me Romans 8.28: "For we know that *all* things work together for good to those who love God, who are the called according to His purposes." Looking back now, I realise that I was truly angry with God for the first time in my life. Oh, how patient our Heavenly Father must be with us. He always knows what's best for us, and He knew just what He was doing. How we thanked Him for the gift of our baby daughter, Anita.'

But God hadn't finished teaching us just how near He is, for when Wesley was just six years old illness hit him without warning. Hazel and I were awakened in the middle of the night by his excessively noisy breathing. Something was seriously wrong and we called in our doctor. He was puzzled and made arrangements to rush the bewildered Wesley into the local isolation hospital for further tests.

Hazel and I were, of course, most worried when meningitis was mentioned as a possible diagnosis. This, thankfully, was not the right diagnosis. Nevertheless there was no doubt something was seriously wrong with him. His condition continued to deteriorate, with a paralysis of one side of his face a further complication. His condition puzzled the doctors for a further two weeks as Christmas was fast approaching. Wesley got weaker and weaker. Christmas Eve came and all the children were discharged home except for Wesley and a tiny baby, who knew nothing about the time of year anyway. It was heartbreaking to leave Wesley in hospital that night and Hazel, as she recalls, cried all the way home.

'I felt utter despair, and helplessness. Here was something Mummy couldn't kiss better. All we could do was to cry to the Lord in desperation to do something or we might lose him. Christmas Day dawned and we tried to do Christmassy things for Anita's sake, but our hearts just weren't in it. Wesley was too ill to take much notice of the presents we took in to him. I remember leaving the hospital for a short time to go to the Christmas morning service at our Fellowship. How we praised God for folk like these. Their support and most of all their prayers made such a difference. When we were too tired and distressed even to pray we *felt the prayer and support of Christian friends.*'

It is at these times in our lives that we realise just how weak and helpless we are. We need to go to the One who *is* our Strength. This realisation dawned in a new, fresh, and experimental way and proved to us that our Heavenly Father was available and accessible: He was compassionate and caring; He was a comforter and encourager; and above all a *very present help in time of trouble*!

As a Christian family we had always believed in prayer. But in that time of extreme trouble, trial and stress we learned the difference between just '*saying our prayers*' and really *praying*.

It was a strange Christmas. It was almost as if it didn't exist in that hospital as Wesley fought for his life. He was so weak he couldn't swallow any food and we were close to despair.

Finally in desperation the doctors decided to give him a course of strong steroid drugs, which carried some risks to him, to try and cure him. Back we went again, in earnest, heart-felt prayer for the Lord to intervene and come to our son's aid.

33

Praise God He did! That same day Wesley started to improve, with the help of the hospital staff, but most of all, we're sure, the Lord's help. The tide of illness turned. Progress in the next weeks was slow. He was so thin his clothes just hung on him and he looked for all the world like an orphan depicted in some Victorian children's home. Finally came the day we'd prayed for. He was fit enough to return home.

It didn't matter that Christmas was just a memory in most people's minds. We had our Christmas festivities in February in great delight and abandonment.

Wes is now twenty years old. He's handsome, with a ready wit and winsome character, and a firmly rooted Christian conviction. Those memories of that Christmas fourteen years ago will never pass from the minds of Hazel and me. It was a time when God proved to us that He is available to us, and present not necessarily to deliver us *from* our besetting trials but to see us *through* them. He is always there.

JONI EARECKSON TADA

❧

Joni has inspired millions with her courage and faith in the face of her paraplegia, and some of her life-changing experiences have been captured in the film **Joni**. *She has written a number of books relating faith and life, none more powerful than* **Choices, Changes**, *in which she describes a most unexpected change in her life.*

Joni writes of a Sunday when her church's minister John MacArthur is away and there is a guest preacher.

After the offering, special music and another hymn, the guest speaker climbs the steps to the pulpit. I settle down to listen. He introduces the sermon with a story. It gets a little long and my mind begins to wander. I slap my thoughts back in line. Attention! Front and centre! This a worship service, Eareckson.

My eyes settle on a dark head down front, four or five pews ahead. Thick black hair. My heart skips a beat. It's him. I can't see his face, but I know it's him. How is that he's in church – this church? I strain to see, but . . . no, of course it isn't. It's just someone who looks like him from the back. The tension and adrenaline drain away.

The power of those dormant feelings takes me by surprise, knocks me off balance. From nowhere, I can taste the faint disappointment of old pipe dreams and false hopes.

The man tilts his head slightly, revealing a strong jaw and the smooth tanned curve of his neck. He leans to the left and in profile reaches for a Bible in the back of his pew. Other feelings force their way in –

longings, wishful thinking, regret. Tiny darts of depression pinprick my resistance.

No. No. This must not happen. I will not sit here and squander this worship service on selfish notions! If I can't concentrate on the sermon, I will rivet these irksome thoughts into line – nail them down once and for all. We take captive every thought to make it obedient to Christ. I remember the line from Scripture.

I find, though, that it takes a mountain of effort to pull my eyes away from the back of the man's head. In this instance, I cannot flee. That black hair – my heart knots. OK, OK. I challenge my feelings. If that's the way you want to play, I can stand firm; if that's where the battle is, that's where I'll fight it.

While the speaker drones in the background I throw on my armour. I focus my eyes on the back of this stranger's head.

Oh, Father . . . You desire mercy rather than judgment. Now be merciful to me, a sinner. And bless You for not judging me according to these awful thoughts. Stupid, silly thoughts that distract me from worshipping You. Be merciful and help me win this battle – for Your honour and for the benefit of this man, whoever he is.

I take a deep breath and gain more ground.

Father, if this man knows You, get him deeper into Your Word. Help him to obey. If he's dating somebody, convict him if he's messing around. If he's married, hold him to his vows. Don't let him get away with cheating, even if only in his thoughts. Strengthen him against the Devil and the world with all its temptations. Make prayer a big part of his life, and give him extra joy when he makes a stand for

You. And if there are problems where he works, make his life shine as a real witness to his co-workers. If there is a lingering argument with his mother or father, resolve it, would You? Make his testimony at home consistent with what he believes here in this church.

I stare at the man's head, his hair black and shining, and a wave of peace washes over me as I sense victory within grasp. We're winning, I smile to the Holy Spirit.

Save him if he's not in Your family. Strengthen him. Refine his faith . . . keep him from lies . . . clear up his bad habits . . . assist him in prayer . . . sustain his health . . . guard his mind . . . deepen his friendships . . . make him into the man You want him to be.

My heart is filled with honest-to-goodness joy. I know, through my prayer, that God is being exalted on this Lord's Day, even if in a most unorthodox manner. The speaker is winding up his message. It's too late for me to pick up his drift, so . . .

Almighty God, Father of all mercies . . .

I begin a silent piece of liturgy I've known since I was a child . . .

. . . we, thine unworthy servants do give thee most humble and hearty thanks for all thy goodness and loving kindness to us and to all men. We bless thee for our creation, preservation, and all the blessings of this life. But above all, for thine inestimable love in the redemption of the world by our Lord Jesus Christ, for the means of grace and for the hope of glory.

As the speaker closes his sermon and asks the congregation to rise for the closing prayer, I continue my own petition.

> And we beseech thee, give us that due sense of all thy mercies that our hearts may be unfeignedly thankful, and that we may show forth thy praise not only in our lips but in our lives – by giving up ourselves to thy service and by walking before thee in holiness and righteousness all our days. Through Jesus Christ Our Lord, to whom with thee and the Holy Ghost be all honour and glory, world without end. Amen.

'Amen,' the speaker says from the pulpit, and several in the congregation echo, 'Amen.' It is noon, and digital watches around me beep the hour in unison. The organist pulls out all the stops as the postlude permits everyone to gather sweaters, books and purses. People begin shuffling out of the pews.

'I'm starved. Let's hurry home for lunch,' Judy says as she steps out of the pew and over my footpedals.

'Let's!' I respond, but I am watching the man down front as he steps into the aisle and begins chatting with several people. I consider – only for a moment – approaching and introducing myself, perhaps mentioning my prayer for him. I instantly dismiss the notion. No. He'd think I was nuts! Or making advances or something. Besides, I don't want the morning's victory to be tarnished. I'll keep it between God and me.

A month or so passes. The memory of that morning battle with temptation has faded. I am at another worship service at Grace Church. Afterward, an acquaintance introduces me to a nice looking oriental man. He looks familiar, and I study him with a puzzled air. Brightening, I ask him to turn around. He looks just as puzzled. 'I want to see the back of your head,' I explain. So he complies.

Sure enough, he is the man with the thick, black hair. We laugh when I tell him I prayed for the back of his head just a couple of months ago. I simplify my story, saying something about a boring sermon. We chat for a few moments.

As I start to power my wheelchair towards the exit, I realise I've already forgotten his name, and circle my chair around.

'Ken Tada.' He smiles and waves goodbye.

BOB GILBERT

Bob Gilbert has for many years been at the helm of Methodist, Christian witness in the Armed Forces and he has been based at the Methodist central offices in London at Westminster Central Hall. He has edited the magazine **Over To You***.*

At the end of the War in Europe, HMS Unicorn – the aircraft carrier on which I was serving – moved from the Indian Ocean to the Philippine Islands in the Pacific.

The crew numbered 1400. On board conditions were very cramped and, as the carrier was not designed for the tropics, it was hot and sticky and especially so in the small chapel. Although I used to say my prayers in my hammock, there was so much noise around me it was difficult to concentrate. I found it far better to go up on the vast flight deck where the planes took off and landed, and which at night was nearly always deserted. There, beneath the Pacific moon and stars, I experienced some of the most precious moments I have ever known in my life. They were times when it seemed God was walking with me. His presence was so real and I felt if I put out my hand I could touch Him. At times I found myself running with sheer excitement at this overwhelming sense of His nearness.

I had recently been in America where I was in close fellowship with lively Christian groups. I also knew there were numbers of Christians in fellowship on other ships, and wondered why there was no such group on mine. As far as I knew at that time I was the only Christian on the carrier, though I later met another and no doubt there were others. But looking back on that sense of isolation and aloneness, I realise the Lord used it in a very special way to prepare me for all that lay ahead. The experience helped me to identify with the many folk I have met during my ministry who for one reason or another are alone.

I certainly understood, especially when serving as a chaplain during the Korean War, how we can all meet with God, wherever we are.

It must have been hard for Jesus, in the small peasant home at Nazareth which he shared with brothers and sisters and animals to find a quiet place to pray. This, I think, explains why he spent so much time walking and talking with God on the Galilean hillsides. We also can encounter God at any time and in any place.

RAY GOUDIE

Ray Goudie is mentor of Heartbeat, a Christian rock band who have had several hit records in the British pop charts. The band also take a very active role in general religious activities, especially amongst young people.

There was one precious moment that turned my life upside down.

I had been involved with Christian music for some fifteen years and I had been on the stage of many Christian meetings and knew many of the younger evangelists.

I was at a Spring Harvest gathering and on stage. Luis Palau was giving his testimony. To me it was just another event, nothing more. I believed in Jesus, yes, although I wouldn't say it was a close relationship. But suddenly it hit me – what *was* my faith? I actually wanted to go forward and really accept Jesus, but then the thought of the public spectacle of responding made me sweat like mad and stopped me from giving myself. And yet, I realised that for ten years or so I had lived in a hypocritical way. I knew there and then that God must have His way. I was, I suppose, waiting for a power to hit me. I remember saying to God, 'Please make me strong', and I asked for the Holy Spirit, and I asked for the Spirit's power. I believed and I received and I said 'Thank-you' to God.

When I told my wife Nancy what had happened she was nonplussed. She wondered what had happened to me. I said I had asked God to fill me with His Spirit and He had, and that I had asked God to fill me with confidence. So many marvellous things have happened since then. God did something wonderful to me. When I was willing to open up to Him then He was willing to come in. Nancy knew something major had happened to me, and she, too, yearned for a similar experience. She said she would pray all day and all night until God spoke to her. He did. He amazed her. You see God said to both of us, 'Stop your present life and follow Me, in My way.'

And we said yes.

AMY GRANT

*Amy Grant is a four time Grammy winner and her voice
and songs are known worldwide. Amy has been one of the
very few singers who have found success in the general music
world after first finding acceptance in the 'Jesus Music' and
white gospel idioms. She grew up on a farm in Nashville,
started writing songs when she was fifteen, and was signed
to **Word Records** shortly after.*

Popularity does change things in some ways. People
do stare at you but I can go out and not be mobbed,
and I can go to a movie and be relaxed, though
sometimes it is hard. All of a sudden, when you
become somebody, people start making value
judgments and sometimes they find you are not the
person they think you are. I don't think I would like
someone to try to make me into a superstar. I think
they would fail miserably. I think you have to have
a certain flavour to your personality to be a superstar,
and I just don't think I have that. I get frightened when
someone thinks they have a corner on my life. I get
worried if I think people are asking more of me than
they're asking of themselves. I have to admit, though,
that since I'm in the public eye and have chosen to be
there, my life will be lived under a magnifying glass,
at least in some respects.

It hasn't been easy taking myself from a religious
music world to the music scene as a whole and at very
least trying to convince some people that I've not
forgotten my past. When I signed with A & M I asked
why they signed me. They said they signed me as an
artist. They said 'We want you to be you' and 'so long

as you pay the rent, you can have time to write songs!'

I'm fortunate that I'm a songwriter, although of course I do sing other people's songs. When it comes to choosing my songs there are five of us who vote! We sit around and play tapes of demo songs that are submitted by others or simply ones we have come across and I sing my songs. All in all it means a lot of work. It helps, of course, that I know some songwriters well, such as Michael Smith whose music I like a lot. You know sometimes it can be just me who wants to do a particular song, and this was the case with one song that has proved so popular, 'Saved By Love'. On the demo, it really hadn't sounded too good. The song meetings at the farm are fun. Sometimes when there is doubt about a song I stay with it for a bit and then we might all agree that it's OK.

All these moments have made life so precious. It is so precious to have found such love from my husband, too. But of course, I had the right start in life. I had a Christian upbringing in a closely knit family and I've always been led into good ways. I was aware of Jesus from an early age.

I thank God for allowing me to sing. I've experienced so many marvellous things. Once in Atlanta five thousand kids lit candles, then got up from their seats and sang together. I have had so many moments of truth, but there is one very precious and special moment which happened in 1973.

Like I said, I grew up among Christian things. I heard and I sang about Christian faith from my very early years, and I didn't ask questions. It all seemed so right and true. Then, there does come the time when you ask what it means and I knew I must know Jesus for myself.

So it was that in 1973 I was baptised. I just let go and went down on my knees. It was my finding and my commitment, so I was moving from learnt faith to knowing faith. For me, it was another few years before I was really swimming. I'm still with Jesus, praise His Name!

FRED PRATT GREEN

❧

Fred Pratt Green has become one of the most exciting twentieth-century hymn writers with his material appearing in new denominational hymn collections. In his eighties, and still very active, he lives in Norwich. He is a minister of the Methodist Church in Britain.

It happened when I was nineteen years of age and on holiday with my parents in Brittany. I was in a very troubled state of mind. If you are to understand why, I must fill in for you my family background.

My parents were typical Victorians. They had lifted themselves, like so many others, out of very humble circumstances into the middle class by hard work and native intelligence. By the time I was born, much the youngest, my father had established a prosperous leather goods manufacturing business in Liverpool, then a booming city. He owed much of his success to my mother, who was gentle and loving, as tough as nails, and thrifty. My sister, fifteen years older than myself, and my brother, nine years older, went into the family business; it was expected that my brother would take over the business when my father eventually retired.

Then, just as I was about to leave my minor public school with my exact future (possibly in architecture) still in doubt, something quite appalling happened. My brother, after a final row with my father – they couldn't get on because they had the same temperament – kicked over the traces, left the firm and set up in opposition, opening a little factory not half a mile away. It came as a complete shock to me.

49

My mother was far more upset than I had ever seen her. It was natural that my father, in these circumstances, should turn to me. He clearly expected me to take my brother's place. But such gifts as I had, as my school reports showed, were literary and artistic; deep-down I knew I had no stomach for factory life and for business management. On the other hand, I sympathised with my father and wanted to please him. It was an emotional situation. Keeping my fears to myself, I consented to go into the business. My father was delighted and generous. So I went to work, first of all learning the trade in the factory and then acting as secretary of our retail shop in the centre of Liverpool. Every morning, as my father and I walked to the station to go by underground, my brother passed us on the other side of the road, walking to the ferry.

But during this time, something else was happening to me. My parents regularly attended a Wesleyan chapel in Wallasey, and here I came under the influence of a minister who was both a man of culture and an evangelist. One Sunday night I responded to an appeal, following a sermon on John Masefield's 'Everlasting Mercy', and quickly became a committed Christian. It wasn't long before my minister thought I ought to become a local preacher. Is it to be wondered at that having won acceptance as a local preacher I was urged to consider the ministry? I began to feel I had the necessary 'call'. Only my mother knew what was in my mind; my father was not the kind of man to whom one could easily talk. I knew he would be angry and hurt if, like my brother, I deserted him. I was tortured by the need to come to a decision, one way or the other. Neither my mother nor my minister, however sympathetic, could tell me what to do.

It was at this point that my father decided on a motoring holiday in Brittany. A car was hired and an employee acted as chauffeur.

So, one day in 1922, we drew up in a Breton village. I was free to sketch. After sketching the village calvary, I went into the church. It was a surprisingly humble place, small and dark, the dampness of centuries mingling with a faint aroma I knew to be incense. There was a strangeness and a mystery about the place I found impressive. In a corner an old woman lit a candle and then knelt down. I waited. She got up and clattered out. Something impelled me to take her place, to light a candle, and to kneel. It was easy to pray. I poured out my story to Christ, to God. Then I sat on a bench, not praying, but comforted. Odd thoughts came and went. Something reminded me of Saint Francis of Assisi – how, compelled to choose between obedience to his earthly father (and a life of ease) and poverty, he had chosen poverty as his vocation.

When I went out into the sunlight I was startled to find I had been an hour in that church, to which I cannot even give a name, and I knew I had to offer for the ministry.

As soon as I could I broke the news to my mother.

'You must tell your father,' she said. 'Then, leave it to me.'

It was many months before my father was reconciled to the fact that his younger son would not carry on the family business. At last, after a service in my home church which, as a candidate for the ministry, I was permitted to conduct, he went to the porch, as if he were the preacher, and shook hands with the departing congregation. 'Hasn't my son done well!' he said, over and over again. In my father's book, I was a success.

Thus began what has been my 'providential way'. I am sceptical enough to question a young man's emotional experience as evidence of divine guidance, but cannot deny the evidence of a lifetime, not least in twenty years of a retirement of wholly unexpected opportunity.

TINA HEATH

*Tina Heath is an actress and television presenter, particularly well known for working on **Blue Peter**. She is married to singer-songwriter and composer Dave Cooke, who apart from his own work spent some years backing Cliff Richard.*

There have been a number of significant 'moments' in my life but I suppose one of *the* most significant occurred when a very dear friend of ours died, very suddenly, and at an early age. Dave and I found it very hard to accept sympathy or well-meaning friends' explanation of what had taken place. We were not sure whether or not he had known the Lord. We wanted desperately to know where he was. After several days of total deafening silence from heaven (or so it seemed) I remembered one Scripture which would not go away. It was 'I am the Living One; I was dead and behold I am alive for ever and ever! And I hold the keys of death and hell.'

I quickly looked up the passage (Revelation 1. 17–18) and also read the preceding verses 12 to 17. They had tremendous impact on me as I realised how great and mighty and all-powerful Christ is. I knew in that moment that our dear friend would have come face to face with Jesus at his moment of death because Jesus holds death's keys! I knew that I could trust Jesus with our friend's destiny, because Jesus is really and truly Lord of heaven and hell and all of his judgments are loving, just and right.

We still miss our friend very much, but are at peace, even though we don't know the outcome of his certain encounter with Christ.

GARTH HEWITT

~

Garth Hewitt has been very much to the fore in what has been termed the 'Jesus Music' world. He is a Christian and many of his songs have a direct Christian input. In his music he raises certain questions in people's minds about life and truth, and at the same time he wants to get across something positive about Jesus. In recent years he has been very much involved in raising money for Tear Fund and arousing in Christians and others greater political and social awareness. He has been one of the major figures behind the spectacularly successful Greenbelt Festival.

Garth Hewitt's marriage of words with a variety of musical styles (including blues, country, rock and rock 'n' roll) comes from a reflective and ever-growing biblical awareness. For some time he had to throw off an unintended 'gimmick' image — people assumed that because he was a clergyman and sang songs he could be labelled 'the singing parson' or 'the rocking vicar'. He says quite simply, 'I'm a clergyman, and I don't treat that as a gimmick. I'm also a singer and a songwriter and I don't treat them as a gimmick either.'

He talks of several moments of truth that have been formative in his later Christian musical expression. He remembers his time at university.

'About that time I had read a book called Tortured By Christ which was about various Christians who suffered for their faith in a Rumanian jail, and I thought if their faith (and the faith I had known) was just a myth, at least it was a myth that worked! And as I looked back on my own life and the way in which God had worked in the past, I realised I had to dismiss this either as a coincidence or a figment of my imagination. Or, alternatively, He really had been there and He had worked. I found it was very hard simply to write it off as a coincidence. That was ignoring the facts.'

He found himself rediscovering faith. Another moment of truth was to follow almost instantly. Dr Francis Shaeffer came to lecture at the university.

'As he spoke, I realised that the Christian message is not only something which is intellectually acceptable, it's the clearest picture that fits the whole world in which we live! I began to realise that it's not good enough simply that Christianity should work.'

It led to Hewitt poring over the Scriptures and seeing the Bible afresh. 'I realised the most fantastic thing was that it was true. I could trust it! It was reliable! Since then I have increasingly found that as I've read the Bible there is nothing that speaks more clearly to our world and situation!'

Some years later he found himself listening to a professor from the Free University of Amsterdam, talking about the death of Christ. 'The professor's theme was that Jesus Christ did not die simply to make us Christians – that's not enough. He died to make us humans! I think that is very profound.' From this insight has sprung Hewitt's subsequent worldwide Christian ministry that has grown and grown in the late 1980s, with his increasing concern to see the Gospel permeating social and political realities. He says, 'Often an evangelist's lifestyle can look very unreal. That's why during my chatter in between my songs I try to be honest and really human, so that people see this is a guy who blows his nose, goes to the loo, wakes up bleary-eyed, has his down-days and all the other sort of things that happen to everyone – and yet has discovered the truth about Jesus Christ!'

GLENN HODDLE

Glenn Hoddle found fame and fortune playing for the North London football team Tottenham Hotspur. He has been capped on numerous times for England but many people think his true skills have been ill rewarded by the sometimes seemingly random nature of England's soccer tactics and team selections. These days he plays for Monaco.

For many a teenager idolising the amazing football skills of England-capped Glenn Hoddle, there must be total unawareness that such a gifted sportsman might feel he had few answers to the central problems of life and living. After all, would they not say that football skill and success constitute the very essence of a happy existence?

Glen certainly gave no clues that it might be otherwise, although some of those close to him knew he had once attended a dinner arranged by Christians In Sport that had taken place at White Hart Lane, the home of Tottenham Hotspur, and the club for which Glenn played. On this occasion he had met Cliff Richard; it had even been arranged beforehand that the two would find themselves next to each other at the dinner. Glenn was impressed by Cliff's words and soon after that he began to read the Bible, but he had so many demands on his time that he ceased doing so. So he put out of his mind the basic question that applies to every human being: 'What is the purpose of my life?'

Glenn's next contact with Christian matters lay six years on and this time it happened not through the efforts of Christians In Sport but simply as a by-product of his footballing career. The month was February, the year 1986, and he was part of the England squad for the World Cup finals that would take place the same year in Mexico. England found Israel an agreeable nation with whom they could lay the basis of pre-World Cup preparation. The team journeyed to the Middle East and during their stay they were taken to see Jerusalem and then to Bethlehem. Glenn was absolutely thrilled by what he saw. He had always seen Jesus as an important historical figure in a much told story, but no more than that. Now Jesus began to emerge as a highly relevant person for life in the present, especially for *his* life.

Once more Glenn read through the New Testament, and the rest is newspaper history . . . for once there was a whiff that he had become a Christian, the newspaper writers were hot on the scent.

No one likes intrusion upon their personal life. But in this instance Glenn could not keep quiet, for the need to tell his moment of truth was strong. He felt he had walked blind for years and now he could see.

PROVOST R.T. HOWARD

*In his book **Ruined and Rebuilt**, Provost Howard recounts both crucifixion and resurrection in this moving and positive description of some events that happened in 1940, and which have been recalled and remembered.*

When the German air force left the coast of France on 14th November, 1940, the fate of Coventry and its cathedral was written in the stars; for it was a brilliant night, a bomber's dream. Towards eight o'clock, the first incendiaries struck the cathedral.

Soon the whole interior was a seething mass of flames and piled-up blazing beams and timbers, interpenetrated and surmounted with dense bronze-coloured smoke . . . All night the city burned, and her cathedral burned with her – emblem of the eternal truth that, when men suffer, God suffers with them. Yet the tower still stood, with its spire soaring to the sky – emblem of God's overruling majesty and love.

By early morning the destruction was complete. Every roof was gone and the whole cathedral lay open to the sky. The matchless pillars, chancel and aisles were lying on the ground in long piles of broken masonry . . .

It was as if a thousand years of natural decay had come upon the cathedral in a single night. But, as the morning grew, and a pale sun caressed the ruins, sounds reached it from the striken city. The sound of crane and hammer and shovel, clearing new arteries, of voices shepherding evacuees, of the rhythm of workshop and factory. It was the people of Coventry piecing together their shattered home, making a new future, strengthened by the ordeal they had shared with their beloved cathedral.

As I watched the cathedral burning, it seemed to me as though I were watching the crucifixion of Jesus upon His Cross. After all, the cathedral was not primarily a church belonging to man; it was the church of Jesus Christ. That such a glorious and beautiful building, which had been the place where Christian people had worshipped God for five hundred years, should now be destroyed in one night by the wickedness of man, was such a monstrous evil that nothing could measure it. It was in some way a participation in the infinite sacrifice of the crucifixion of Christ.

As I went with this thought in my mind the deep certainty arose that as the cathedral had been crucified with Christ, so it would rise again with Him. How, or when, we could not tell; nor did it matter. The cathedral would rise again . . .

The new cathedral is now finished; it stands beside the ruins of the old, and both together declare to the world this immortal truth — that in all of human experience united with Jesus Christ, painful and sorrowful crucifixion will issue in joyful and glorious resurrection.

LAVINE HUDSON

~

Lavine Hudson is the daughter of a Pentecostal minister. In recent years she has become regarded as one of the most exciting gospel singers on the British religious scene. Lavine was signed by Virgin Records, a general record company with wide distribution throughout the world. Press coverage for Lavine has been enormous. However, people need not fear that she is compromising her beliefs for, as this quotation from the magazine **Time Out** *clearly shows, this girl's not for buying. 'She is equally unimpressed by artists who "doctor" pop songs to appeal to a gospel market as by gospel songs whose lyrics are deliberately made ambiguous for appeal to the pop market. "You've got to be straight about it. You should be direct. That was another problem with recording companies. They said, 'You can do gospel but just take Jesus out of it.' I mean, what's the point?" '*

Gospel isn't just music – it's a way of life. I'm a live performer, I can sing and I relate to what I believe. In the music world people always want you to fit into a category, to take you over and tell you what you should or should not do. You can become a used person.

I'm a determined person. I'm not stubborn, though some people think I am. I have a clear idea of what I should be doing and I resist people who want to water down what I do, so such people will find me difficult. I like following my work through and not everyone finds that comfortable when they are a producer. And music is for the heart.

I don't want to be a star – gospel is what I'm doing. I just put on a nice outfit, go out there and sing. I won't play clubs. I can't dance and I don't plan to start. I don't want to be dressed by other people or have my career mapped out by them.

As for my precious moment, well, I was in the States and I had no money, no job, no visa. I had a college place in a top music school, at Berkeley. There was no money for my keep and in no way was I coming home to beg from my cousins. They were in no position to help me.

I had to get down on my knees and pray. You know, the next day I got a call and I was asked how much I needed . . . and there it was!

I pray a lot and ask for strength and I find answers in many ways – sometimes not in the way I expected. Sometimes I've not been able to kneel physically but you have to get down there in your heart.

TONY JASPER

~

Tony Jasper is an author, journalist and broadcaster and has worked extensively in these fields, as well as in drama and sport. He is a double graduate in Theology, is a lay preacher and has led conferences and meditations in a variety of settings, from house churches to more traditional mainstream Christian gatherings.

My mother told me that my Aunt Bess was very ill. No one knew how long she would live. It could be days, even several weeks. She was over 300 miles away. I prayed about what I should do. I was as ever very busy, uncertain whether I should go and see her the following day or perhaps at the end of the week . . .

I rang a minister friend of mine. He said I should go as soon as possible. I decided I would go the next day and tried to clear my diary.

On the Saturday I left a little after seven for the six hour journey by bus and train. I hadn't told anyone I was coming. Somehow it had slipped my memory, what with the endless phone calls that had had to be made.

A few months before this I had completed a new book, *The Illustrated Family Prayer Book*, and I had dedicated it to Bess and my other splendid Aunties. I had told her of this, but had wondered if she would ever see the dedication or book. However, on the Friday I had learned from the publishers that some copies had come into the office, and on hearing my story they had said they would dispatch one right away to her. So I sat on the train and wondered if it would arrive in time, although I knew that my Aunt might well live for several more weeks.

My stay would be short for I had a preaching engagement on Sunday; and so, with the train arriving a little before one, I would be on my way back by late afternoon. I sat on the train and worried, for if the train broke down I might be faced with an awkward situation. But I prayed that my thoughts would dwell on God, on Jesus . . .

British Rail delivered me on time. The walk from the station took ten minutes, and as I neared the house – for my Aunt had insisted she would leave this life from where she lived – I could see my mother outside talking with someone. My mother looked worried, very strained and anxious. Suddenly she noticed me and for a moment it was as though she had seen a ghost. Then she said my name and we embraced. She told me Bess was very bad and that she might not last more than a day or so, but she was still sometimes conscious and aware.

I reached the bedroom, opened the door, and there she was – eyes open, and a smile on her face. She simply said, 'I knew you would come', and we kissed and gazed. How that look seemed to eat me up, as though all of me had to be something for that one moment.

My mother had come into the room and told Bess I had come a long way just for her, but I don't think a thought about length and time passed her way. There was a pause and then I saw *the book* on her bed! It had come and she had looked through it, somehow.

She took my hand and asked me to pray a prayer from the book. I was for a moment at sea, not knowing what words, which words, any words. I couldn't read.

To my surprise, she had found one. She pointed to

it, and for a few seconds she seemed possessed with enormous strength, given the authority that had come her way from being a hospital Sister and then Matron of a large home.

I gazed at the words and for a moment I remember almost lurching forwards, unable to speak them; and then I was quietened by a force from outside me. And there, with someone dying from cancer, perhaps minutes, hours, away from the great divide, I was to say:

This is another day, O Lord. I know not what it will bring forth, but make me ready, Lord, for whatever it may be. If I am to stand up, help me to stand up bravely. If I am to sit still, help me to sit quietly. If I am to lie low, help me to do it patiently. And if I am to do nothing, let me do it gallantly. Make these words more than words, and give me the Spirit of Jesus, Amen.

Yes, it is one thing to compile anthologies in the comparative seclusion of a working room, another to see those words given real flesh where they count and have to count.

She smiled, and we embraced once more, each looking at the other long and lovingly. Her eyes closed and she lay there. I rose from my knees, on to which I had fallen to read the prayer, and was beginning to leave the room, when again she opened her eyes and spoke: 'Death is nothing really.'

She died the next day but never regained consciousness after that moment. It was a precious moment.

PAUL JONES

*Paul Jones was well-known as the lead singer of **Manfred Mann** and is now lead vocalist of **The Blues Band**. He starred in the West End hit musical **Kiss Me, Kate** and has numerous credits in radio and TV. His is married to the popular actress Fiona Hindley.*

Back in 1967 Paul Jones, lead singer of the popular group Manfred Mann, appeared on a television programme called *Looking For An Answer*. He had recently starred in the film *Privilege*, playing a pop star cynically exploited by religion.

The TV show began by showing clips from the film *Privilege* and clips of Cliff Richard taking part in a Billy Graham crusade at London's Earl's Court.

This was a cue for the programme's presenter Robert Kee to ask, 'Is the Church exploiting Cliff Richard too?' It was mildly suggested that Cliff was 'using' his mass pop acceptance and general public platform to persuade people they should become Christians.

There seemed little real dialogue between the two famous pop stars. Jones was cynical, feeling that Cliff (and Billy Graham) were using mass hysteria. Jones told Cliff, 'Right, so you say you're giving them Christ. Well, I say you're not, you're giving them a show.'

But the future would hold an unexpected sequel, in Jones's own Christian conversion during the mid-eighties. In 1967 there had been a clash of pop stars with different ideas about the meaning of self, truth, life, and ultimate reality. Today, they share a common faith, and as well as frequent personal contact, Paul took part in Cliff's summer gospel tour of 1989, and the two of them, along with Paul's wife, Fiona Hindley, gave their testimonies during the Billy Graham campaign meetings in London, in the summer of 1989.

Paul's moment of truth came in unexpected fashion. He became interested in the paintings of Caspar David Friedrich, a rather obscure eighteenth-century German artist. Jones had spotted his paintings during a German tour by the Blues Band, a worthy outfit formed by Jones in the eighties.

'I would stare for hours at Friedrich's paintings,' he says. He found the German artist's work expressive of a definite spirituality. 'I think now that it was because the pictures were painted by someone whose love for Jesus was very, very strong.'

Soon he was in the right frame of mind and attitude to explore in greater depth the faith he had once ridiculed. And so it was that during a Luis Palau meeting at the Queen's Park Rangers football ground he felt he must commit himself to Jesus. In this he was joined by his actress girlfriend, Fiona.

Caspar David Friedrich could never have imagined that his paintings would help to turn someone's life completely around and few, if any, of those who watched the Paul Jones versus Cliff battle of 1967 could have dreamt that one day the two would walk hand in hand with the same Lord.

GORDON LANDRETH

Gorden Landreth spent fourteen years as Administrative Officer in the British Civil Service. He became Graduate Secretary of what was then known as the IVF (Inter Varsity Fellowship), which supported Christian witness in the universities. For the period 1969 to 1982 he became General Secretary of the Evangelical Alliance. In more recent time he was appointed Administrator of Trinity College, Bristol and is at present Co-ordinator of the British Students International Centre, Bristol.

I went overseas in the Army just after the end of the Second World War, to the Middle East, and this gave me a taste for overseas service, even if the experience as a Royal Engineer in Palestine at the end of the British mandate was not always entirely pleasurable. There were two of us subalterns who went up together from our base camp in Egypt to Palestine: I went to the north and the other chap to the south. A few months later I heard my colleague had been killed dealing with a mine on a railway line. I found myself wondering why I had escaped without serious incident coming my way, though others in the unit were involved in 'terrorist' incidents against us as the controlling power.

When I was demobbed I returned to Oxford to complete my degree and as I sought the Lord's guidance for my vocation I felt a concern to work in a secular job overseas, as what we called a 'non-professional missionary'. It seemed to me that there was a real need for some of us Christians with the qualifications to work as government officers in the Inter Varsity Missionary Fellowship for the 'professional' missionaries. I applied for a number of jobs – in the Foreign Service, the Sudan Civil Service and the Colonial Service. I was offered a job in the Colonial Service and had a sense of peace that this was the most suitable for me and that my prayers for guidance had been answered. My year's training course at Cambridge confirmed that sense of rightness and I went abroad to Nyasaland (as Malawi was then called) feeling sure I was in the place the Lord wanted me.

After eight years in Nyasaland I had cause to thank God for a sense of His presence and guidance when pressure in the time of civil emergency was very heavy and even some I thought were my friends were critical. It was the time in 1958/9 when the imposition of the Federation of the three territories of Northern and Southern Rhodesia and Nyasaland caused a backlash from the African Congress in Nyasaland under Dr Banda and various civil disturbances broke out which I, as District Commissioner in Karonga in the far north of the country, had to contain in my areas as my colleagues in the other districts did in theirs. We were extremely stretched in the Northern Province and I had only about a dozen police for the whole area. On one occasion we arrested a particular trouble-maker, but in the face of a large and hostile crowd had to let him go. In an atmosphere of tension and some fear it was good that that particular weekend we were starting a small Bible study group for a few of us expatriates on our station where there were about half a dozen such families. I recall that meeting as an oasis of trust and confidence in God at a time of great uncertainty.

A short time later things got worse and I found myself supported by an imported platoon of riot police from neighbouring Tanganyika. A state of emergency had just been declared and some political ringleaders taken into detention. A hostile crowd was advancing on the government headquarters and I had the unenviable job of 'reading the riot act' to the crowd in the vernacular. They continued to advance and the police had to open fire, causing at least one death.

It was a time of great heart-searching for me as the senior government officer in the district. I was helped by a local missionary who felt I was being soft on one of the other expatriates who was working as a special constable, who had been rather sadistic in his handling of one of the local people a few days after the riot. I considered, however, that the main job at the time was to maintain a sense of law and order and that discipline of this individual would have to wait until things were more under control. In the loneliness of having to take this kind of decision my faith was a great support to me, and I had a confidence that, having committed things to the Lord, I could be at peace regarding my actions in spite of facing some tough dilemmas.

MARGARET LISTER

Margaret Lister spent some of her life living in America, but mostly she has been resident in Britain. She has been plagued with one illness after another but in spite of her many pains and dark days she has fought her way through and proclaims soundly that her Lord is with her, whatever happens. She lives in Sheffield.

Sometimes people have to suffer before they look to our Father and I feel this is true of myself; yet God has not given us the spirit of fear, but of power, love and a sound mind.

My health has troubled me on many occasions. One day I haemorrhaged and I was rushed to hospital. I had a lump, and in the end I had a hysterectomy. My heart was broken. I was very anaemic. I didn't know what to do. I suppose I should have said I had beautiful care in hospital. Well, I did, but I kept saying 'Why me?' Before surgery I remember it was a nightmare. I went into the bathroom and I thought of Jesus and I thought of his crucifixion, and I thought I could identify with Him. I was so terrified and would have run away if it was possible. The operation went without any problems and I wanted to be discharged as soon as possible although there was an infection. I just wanted to go home. So I did go, saying, 'God, please get me through this.'

Shortly after, my father had a heart attack and he began to collapse. It happened several times and each time he was whisked off to hospital by ambulance. We began to be very concerned for him. Anyway, he had to retire from work. His birthday is in January and I thought I would request something for him to hear on the radio, but it struck me (I don't know why) that he might never hear it. I felt it was a strange thing to think.

My dad stood tall, had very big hands and was very lovable. He was a beautiful ballroom dancer and had a love for gardening. Oh, he had humour but at times he had a nasty temper.

His health got worse and he coughed blood and they said he had chronic bronchitis. Then they found a patch on his lung and they said he would need cobalt treatment. I kept wondering how much he knew and tried to look on the bright side of things. The doctor was a kindly man and I was shattered by what he said for it appeared the carcinoma was extensive. I recall sitting in the waiting room for a long time. Eventually I made my way home and somehow tried to be normal by wishing everyone a happy Christmas, but deep down I was asking how I would tell everyone Dad would die. I didn't want to accept it.

I broke the news gently to my mother but she didn't say anything. They brought Dad home and it was a few days later, in the early hours of morning, that Mum awoke me and said Dad had haemorrhaged and choked to death. It was three days before his birthday. My mother was wonderful through this and everything which followed. Yes, she was broken-hearted, but she was also strong. A minister came – one I hadn't met before – and he seemed to know a lot about my father. He was a young fellow, very sweet and kind. He talked to me. He got on his knees and he held my hand and said a prayer I don't recall, and then I do remember he said 'Thank you, Jesus', and gently shook me, and he said the same words again. I didn't say anything and he left. Inwardly I was so hurt, so angry. 'Who do I need to thank?' I thought. But I had a lot to learn and it took a while before I did. I was very bitter. The things I feared most had happened to someone near me. In my own illness I felt I was beyond human help and with Dad's death I felt that was true of him and more so of myself.

Each year I receive a Christian calendar and on the evening Dad died I looked at it, trying to find some words of comfort. It was a very strange thing for the words of the day were those of Jesus: 'I am the resurrection and the life. He that believeth in me shall never die.'

Dad was buried on his sixty-fifth birthday. I remember asking the minister if he thought I could call the radio station and tell them about Dad but still ask for the record, his special birthday request. The minister thought they wouldn't think it strange. I wondered what it was I was trying to prove – perhaps that love was stronger than death and that maybe we were not really separated. I called the station and the DJ was very understanding. He played the request and so we celebrated Dad's birthday just the same.

That morning I woke up at four o'clock and I was amazed that it seemed so light at that time, in January. Then I noticed there appeared to be a bright light in the corner of my room where I always hung the calendar. There was a beautiful light surrounding the calendar picture of Jesus. I felt a Presence. I heard inside me a voice saying, 'Your father lives', and a feeling of peace passed over me. I thought, 'No one will believe this.' It was such a precious moment, a moment of truth. Yes, Jesus is the Resurrection and the Life.

GEOFF MANN

~

Geoff Mann is a talented musician and singer-songwriter. He was once with the EMI-contracted group Twelfth Night. He felt he was called into the Christian ministry and, after training, had a curacy in the North of England. He still records, with his band The Bond and as a solo artist.

The moment of truth in my life came at one point in 1980, when I heard God tell me that Christ died for me. If you don't like 'heard', then say 'inwardly perceived' or 'received communication that gave, of itself, complete understanding'. Personally, I find 'heard' perfectly adequate. I call it 'the' moment of truth quite deliberately. When I understood that 'Christ died for you' was a truth directly for me, it made sense of all that I had hoped and longed for up to that point. Does life have any real meaning? Does it matter, ultimately, whether I have lived or not? Is there a God? How can I know? Who is responsible for evil and suffering? Me? God? Anyone? What is truth? In understanding that 'Christ died for you' isn't an anagram, a crossword puzzle clue but is a statement of fact, meaning exactly what it says, all these things were put into the beginning of a perspective. It was as if I had been pulled through myself into a deeper life, a larger life where all further understanding could be found. There was the centre and solidity of truth around which other things would eventually find their rightful orbits. I knew that my new understanding involved commitment of some kind, because Christ's death for me and his life in me had become the real establishment and foundation of my life as a human being. From that moment the reordering of my life in Christ has gone on apace, yet nothing 'heard', 'seen', or understood since then has been more than a facet of its unfolding within me. Jesus is alive, He sends His Holy Spirit, He loves me as I am and so loves me into change and growth. Failure is not defeat because death has been conquered, conquered when Christ died for us. He laid down this most precious and meaningful life to provide for us a bridge from death into life, that God might be all in all. It is because truth is not *our* creation that we can experience it. It is because truth is part of God's nature that we can know Him. It is in accepting Christ's death for us that we begin. Thank God!

LAURIE MELLOR

*Laurie Mellor is widely experienced as a musician, writer and producer in both mainstream and Christian music worlds. He has played alongside groups like Cream and Fairport Convention, and was for some time the bass player with the colourful Ishmael United, latterly Rev Counta and the Speedoze. He is on the Leadership Team of New Life Church, Littlehampton. He has written **A Desert Song**, which considers whether Christians should be involved in rock music.*

I remember back in 1976 that I had a very special encounter with God. I had been drifting away from Him for some months, and experienced a nervous breakdown whilst on holiday. On returning home and having put things right with God and recommitted myself to following Him, I had the most incredible experience of His presence one evening. I can't really remember whether I was awake or asleep, but just remember God being so close that I was carrying on a personal conversation with Him for some hours, and it was just as if He was in the room with me.

It was as if he was sharing some of His secrets with me and as if I was being taken into His confidence. I began to understand how exciting and big His purposes were for mankind and how privileged I was to be part of these plans. It's very difficult to put this into words, but I am sure anyone who has had a similar experience will know what I mean!

JOHN MOTSON

John Motson, the son of a Methodist minister, is best known as the long-surviving football commentator on the BBC Television programme **Match Of The Day**. *He frequently does the commentary for football internationals and the FA Cup Final.*

Why did I think John Motson was a football commentator and no more? I thought of him as a voice, but not as a football boffin and enthusiast. And how wrong I was.

John Motson is a football brain, a fast-talking encyclopedia of Britain's most-watched sport. His study is shelved with football books, magazines and pictures. Only his own football playing skills leave something to be desired. Unlike his fellow BBC commentators such as Jimmy Hill and Bob Wilson he has never played at professional game level.

He stands around five feet seven inches, slightly built, personable, intelligent, amusing and even modest. Early in his life he became a sports reporter for Sheffield's daily, *The Morning Telegraph*, and from there he gravitated to BBC Radio Sheffield. Soon Motson was booked for sport on Radio 2 and with his knowledge and enthusiasm, journalistic skills and distinctive voice it seemed apt that he should audition for the highly rated BBC television programme, *Match Of The Day*. This was in 1971, and within weeks he was part of the regular team alongside Barry Davies and Brian Coleman.

'It's been a long haul really but I'm very much part of a team and that's how we work. A great many people play their part to get games "live" or in edited form on to the screen. I'm very fortunate, for football is my abiding passion and unlike other hobbies which people have, this one sees me paid! And, of course, I travel a great deal both here in Britain and overseas.'

He makes it clear that what he does is far from easy and indeed in those early years of the seventies he wondered if he would make the grade. But he persevered, worked hard and won the day.

Among the skills he must possess there is enthusiasm, an ability to remain interesting, the learning of names and a wealth of detail and anecdote that will both inform and entertain the viewer.

'We all make gaffes. I remember speaking to the magazine *Crusade* (now *Today*) and I told them how I once said, "For those watching in black and white, Spurs are playing in yellow." '

John doesn't talk so much of a moment of truth but more about how religious faith has always been part of his approach to living. He has shied away from being presented in public as the *Match Of The Day* star commentator who is a Christian. He has no objection to the fact of his faith being made known but would rather avoid some of the razzmatazz that could come his way. In some ways he is a very public person but in other things he would wish to reserve some privacy and has no desire to be some kind of public religious exhibit. However, he knows other people take a different perspective.

But he does say, 'As I get older, I become more and more convinced that Christian doctrine is the right one.'

And should he one day hang up his footballing voice, then he says he might well choose to become involved in a Christian cause or movement. He feels he lives close to his Lord so that the whole of living can be *the* time of truth.

LEONARD PEARCEY

~

Although now described as a 'writer and broadcaster', Leonard Pearcey's early days in Religious Broadcasting were as a singer who graduated to being a presenter. In fact, he is the only person to have been both soloist and later presenter on **Songs of Praise***. His work in arts administration led him into arts broadcasting and he now runs the Radio Times BBC Radio and Television Drama Awards and Radio Comedy Awards. His business experience brought him to producing and presenting awards ceremonies, conferences and the like. He was educated at Christ's Hospital and Corpus Christi College, Cambridge.*

Quite early on in my career in Religious Broadcasting I realised that for me the Truth was to be a jigsaw puzzle without a picture on the box and with other people handing me the pieces one at a time.

Each time, producers seemed to point me as a presenter towards a situation in which my areas of doubt acted as a springboard for many questions. Letters from viewers registered appreciation of a broadcaster without total certainty.

As the years passed I found the gradual building up of that certainty exciting, but alarming at the same time: I never quite knew when the next moment of truth would turn up, or at whose hands: because it was always 'third-party', in the course of a meeting perhaps, or an interview . . .

The little boy in Dom Edmund Jones' church at Cockfosters, for example (as an Anglican I always seemed to get many more Catholic or Salvation Army programmes). For someone happy to be in the public eye, I've never really been able to cope with turning in church to shake hands with those around or embrace them or give the sign of the peace. At least I knew that the cameras would be on the congregation as a whole as we turned to clasp hands. I turned to find myself looking down at the tiniest boy with clasped hands raised towards me as high as he could, eyes shining with a happiness and a certainty that brought tears to mine. And, of course, the camera was on me!

Another little boy made me cry inside when I interviewed him and his family at Great Ormond Street for my *Songs of Praise Christmas Special*. He was seriously ill, with a total trust in the future in which his mother joyfully supported him. I felt ashamed of my doubts, but Jonathan gave me a precious and quite large piece of the jigsaw.

Then there was Sheila Hurst, critically ill with cancer, writing wonderful poetry and due to be interviewed by me in Southall in a *Meeting Place* series about facing death. I went to have a chat with her in hospital. I was just back from holiday, bronzed and beautiful they told me, and as I left her room I heard one of the nurses who'd been hiding round the corner say to her, 'Lucky thing – what have you got that we haven't?' 'Cancer,' said Sheila. If you'd said she was courageous she'd have thrown something at you.

You can see the pattern now, the simple expression of the faith of others helping me in my understanding.

One of the many on location Salvation Army programmes I did was a *Seeing and Believing* about their music courses. In between rehearsal and recording we were dining with the officers and being waited on by quite the most attentive waiter I'd ever come across.

'He's well on the way to recovery,' they told me, and I asked for more.

It turned out that this man had had a very serious drug and drink problem and had been sent to them for help. Things were going well, when he suddenly lapsed and ran off. I was amazed that they made no effort to get him back, in fact allowed him to sink even lower. 'We had to let him get to rock bottom, because from that moment on the only way is up.' The logic shocked me, but filled in another gap in the puzzle.

Then in the days when *Thought For The Day* was recorded rather than live, I was part of a series in which a different person each day spoke about a piece of music that meant something special to them. I was speaking on Monday and chose Bilbo's Last Song from the first part of Tolkien's *Lord of the Rings*: 'I sit beside the fire and think of how the world will be when winter comes without a spring that I shall ever see . . .'

It tells of the old hobbit towards the end of his days reflecting contentedly on death just around the corner. I played a record of the Donald Swann setting of the words and related it to death in sunshine and the last time we each without knowing would see a particular loved one or visit a special place.

On Tuesday they played me again by mistake. Hearing your own voice when you're not expecting it is quite a surprise however used you may be to the way you sound on radio, but the biggest surprise was a few days later in a letter from a listener.

She had heard and appreciated my talk on Monday and later that day her brother died unexpectedly and, in having to console his children, she wished she could have heard the item again, knowing that he was gone. 'And the following morning my prayers were granted.'

A strange piece for the jigsaw, that one.

JOHN PERRY

~

John Perry has been a professional musician for over twenty years. For ten years he toured the world as one of the three-man backing vocal group for Cliff Richard. He has been involved in session work and concerts for many other leading music stars including Elton John, Leo Sayer and Shakin' Stevens. Since becoming a Christian in 1979, his personal lifestyle has drastically changed, allowing space for a much greater love for his family and homelife. Since 1986 he has been 'full time' in Christian work, leading worship and giving seminars. He spent five weeks in Hong Kong and worked closely with Jackie Pullinger. He has been a regular contributor at Spring Harvest, Royal Week, Severnside Celebration and Crossfire.

I was working with Cliff and it was the first time that I had done gospel tours. I started to meet people who said they were Christians. I may have met Christians before this, but I hadn't been aware of it particularly. And now we were going on tours with Christian musicians and I found this quite interesting. In some respects I couldn't tell any difference, apart from the fact that there was something about these Christians that I couldn't put my finger on. They were pretty much regular in every other way. They were good players and they did their job all right, but as people there seemed to be something different, something intangible.

Sometimes we had to go to churches and we had to sit through everything, including the sermon, before we got to Cliff's bit. I saw people actually enjoying themselves. I must be honest. I was trying to find out what they were all on about . . . all these kids banging guitars and leaping about and having a good time.

I remember the occasion when I heard a heavy-duty preacher and he seemed to be telling me my life story. I sat there and wondered how he knew all that. I remember the preacher asked people to take the step and ask Jesus into their lives. The trouble was I was sitting next to all my mates. Tony Rivers was there and all the other chaps. It was very embarrassing and, although I wanted to respond, I was too nervous. Then he said people who wanted to respond should put their hands up and my hand went up. I looked at it and said 'Get down'! It was almost like that. The next thing I knew, I was out of my seat and walking down the aisle. There were tears streaming down my face. I was totally wiped out, embarrassment forgotten, a weight off my back. I had not known anything like it. Top to bottom totally cleansed. Brand new. Absolutely beautiful.

MIKE PETERS

*Mike Peters lives in North Wales. He is lead singer of The
Alarm. The group has found considerable success both sides
of the Atlantic. He has made several individual singing visits
to Greenbelt. In the early days of The Alarm, Peters wrote
a song called 'Shout To The Devil', which was his attack
on religion, the Bible and Jesus. When the song appeared
on the group's first album* **Declaration** *in 1983, the words
were changed, because Peter's experience of religion, the Bible
and Jesus had altered. He was beginning to see real truth
in the very faith he had once condemned.*

I received through the post a book that was called
Countdown, which set out the case for Christianity. I
was going to Liverpool for the weekend and I just
remember something in my head saying, 'You mustn't
leave that book behind. You've got to pick it up and
take it with you.' I did and it was a decision that I will
remember for the rest of my life.

All I remember was that the book was saying, 'Do
you want the gift of everlasting life?' I knew I did. The
book explained about belief in a series of questions and
answers that you couldn't deny.

And I just remember having a massive feeling of
release and an overwhelming joy right down deep
inside and I knew I could no longer deny the existence
of Jesus. I was sitting in the middle of a crowded train,
crying my eyes out and deeply happy.

ADRIAN PLASS

Adrian Plass, author of **The Sacred Diary of Adrian Plass,**
*has become one of Britain's best selling writers in the religious
market. His humour and spiritual depth have meant much
to the many thousands who have bought his books.*

When thinking of my childhood, I remember the
tensions at home and my truancy. I wasn't a very lively
truant. I used to go and sit in the park and watch the
old men playing bowls. Or I'd just sit on the
roundabout in the kids' playground and go round and
round, watching my mind revolving really, and get
achingly lonely.

I think if you have problems as a child, especially
if your parents have conflict, you tend to become watchful. You study what happens because you
need to be prepared for disasters – or even happiness.

My father was a Roman Catholic and my mother
went to a Free Church, so they had their own version
of troubles at home, fuelled by my father's intense
jealousy.

I went to church with my father and found it
intensely boring. The only bit I liked was the
communion. I remember seeing their big fleshy
tongues, as they knelt there like baby birds with their
mouths wide open.

My father bought several collections of books and
I used to read everything I could lay my hands on. I
read as though I needed it to live. I used to sit in my
bedroom like someone in a rockpool turning over
stones. I would read Biggles and Conrad side by side

and judge them on their merits, because no one actually guided me.

Then I attended an Anglican youth club. I didn't realise they were actually lusting after my conversion. I used to argue with the curate and he got angrier and angrier as the weeks went by. Finally he stopped being a sort of plastic Christian and he shouted, 'I love you, I love you,' very loudly and banged his fist down on the obligatory formica top bar they had in all sixties Christian clubs. I felt as though I had been punched in the gut, because it was the first real thing he'd said in weeks.

When I was sixteen I made a commitment and settled down to become a sort of hologram Christian. That encounter was real and it always drew me back over long years of aridity. Throughout the following years there was a kind of ironic fondness between God and me. Every now and then I would encounter him around a corner somewhere.

Out of those experiences grew my appreciation of a humorous God, a God who is much nicer, much wiser and warmer and more caring than perhaps we appreciate at times.

DAVE POPE

Dave Pope is a gifted singer-songwriter who has been one of the leading younger evangelists whose work has been richly blessed over the last few years. He is a frequent and popular singer and speaker at major festival gatherings and conventions.

It was a small Methodist chapel in the heart of the industrial West Midlands, and the enthusiastic preacher was looking for all the world like a windmill out of control as he encouraged the congregation to put more effort into their singing. 'Sing out,' he boomed. 'Let your heart respond to God's faithfulness and sound praises to the Lord.' And in true evangelical fashion there was a crescendo in volume and the flock responded to the shepherd, as the lyrics of a 'world-famous' hymn echoed through the building:

> Guide me, O Thou Great Jehovah,
>   Pilgrim through this barren land,
> I am weak, but Thou art mighty,
>   Hold me with Thy powerful hand.

Forgive me if I sound rather cynical at this stage, but at the time the words of that song assumed a distinctly hollow quality, and the gesticulations of an energetic song-leader did nothing to raise my level of faith in God's ability to guide! The yeast had lost its lift – or so I thought. It wasn't that I had abandoned my faith; it was just a huge frustration in waiting for God to show me what He wanted of my life. I had become a Christian as a child, and at the age of sixteen had realised the implications of discipleship. A little later I had responded at a missionary challenge meeting, indicating to the Lord my total availability for service, whatever the cost and wherever the need happened to be. And it was at that point that everything seemed to stand still! Not that I expected to have a confrontation with the Archangel Gabriel in the bathroom the following morning, or that a rose bush would suddenly burst into flames, but I did expect some kind of clear indication that God had a specific purpose and plan for my life and that He would show me the way ahead.

Maybe it was all the more difficult because of my career prospects. University life had whetted my appetite for a future in industrial management and my sponsor had made it clear that I could leave college and take on a senior position in personnel management. Honestly speaking, I found that exciting, but I knew in my heart that it was not God's choice. Whilst studying at university I had been very active in Christian youth work and had seen God's power transform people's lives . . . to the extent that I sensed deeply in my spirit that this was to be part of my life's calling. I was involved in the gospel music scene and my ministry began to develop outside of my immediate locality. Although my interest in college and industry was still important, I knew that God was saying something different and I was eager to take Him at His word – which was why it was all the more difficult to handle the apparent lack of specific guidance when the time came to make decisions. It was all very well for some 'charismatic' preacher to enthuse and gush platitudes, encouraging his people to put their hearts into singing praise to God for His guidance, but what about the reality of all that? As the Americans say,

'What about the rubber hitting the road?'

It was shortly after that frustrating service that I had to make a clear decision. I would either commit myself to industry or become involved in full-time Christian service. My training officer was pushing me for an answer. My heart said one thing, but my head seemed reluctant to fall into line, and so in sheer desperation I cried out to God for real confirmation of His will, admittedly only half expecting an answer!

Over that particular weekend two people I greatly respect quizzed me about my future. 'Ever thought about full-time evangelism?' 'What about the ministry?' This was the substance of the enquiries. 'Maybe coincidence,' I told myself, but the following morning a letter arrived inviting me to join an evangelical mission working amongst students in universities and colleges across the country. Later that day another close friend, himself a minister, encouraged me to apply to another mission looking for someone to help with youth evangelism.

But the real seal came the following day. Our family enjoyed traditional Sunday lunch – usually roast beef and Yorkshire pudding – and inevitably the conversation that particular lunchtime reverted to a discussion of what I was planning to do, I shared what had happened over the previous few days, and then I heard something that was all I needed to hear.

When I was a child I had been taken by my parents to Wolverhampton to a mission meeting and the speaker, Dr Oswald Smith from Toronto, had asked parents who were willing to allow their children to enter Christian ministry to stand at the conclusion of the meeting. My parents had stood up, and as they shared this with me over that Sunday meal it was as if God had given His seal upon the rightness of my commitment to full-time ministry. In one sense, my parents could have shared the story before, but I'm sure I would have been tempted to leave college prematurely, or opt out of the responsibility of study. They could have told me when I was growing impatient and becoming increasingly frustrated, but I would have missed out on learning God's lessons on obedience and waiting on Him.

No, the timing was right, and several years later I had the joy of being in Toronto at the People's Church and sharing the story with the friends there. Oswald Smith attended that service and was tremendously thrilled to hear of how God had used his ministry to confirm my call to evangelism.

'Coincidence,' some would say, but in my mind and understanding this was a distinct and clear 'God incidence' – a special moment of God's grace and an insight into His inestimable faithfulness as He leads His children on.

CLIFF RICHARD

Cliff Richard has had a remarkable show business career that has spanned over thirty years. He had his first pop hit in 1958 and near the end of 1988 was topping the charts in Britain and many other countries of the world. He has had major credits in film and theatre. He is a Christian of over twenty years' standing and has been greatly involved with the relief agency Tear Fund.

I don't know what God has in mind for me but at present I am sure I am doing His will where I am. I can only say, 'Here is me, this is what I am.'

Through being in the pop world I've brought the Christian message to masses of people who would have heard nothing of the Gospel. And on a very practical level I've been partly responsible for founding and then ensuring the success of the Arts Centre Group where Christians in the media can meet, talk and pray together.

I'm constantly thrilled by the Christian faith. It doesn't depend on your emotions. It's a stable and solid factor in my life and it gives me reason to feel confident and positive whatever happens.

I think there is nothing so demanding and so specific. Christianity comes with a Jesus who says He is the only way to God.

There have been many precious moments. I have seen so much growth in a good many areas, often from show-biz people, not known for their spiritual status. It has been a precious moment for me when I have been on stage and I have sung 'When I Survey the Wondrous Cross' – to be there speaking for Jesus.

At the Arts Centre Group I have held special evenings when people from entertainment have come, had some food, talked over things and I have explained my Christian position. Some of these evenings have been my richest moments.

Of course, I have to admit there is always a new generation and some of us older ones have to give way. And young people have to ask questions that have been asked by others − years ago! I think life is always about beginnings. I mean when I am fifty, I shall be saying life begins now. I am conscious there is so much to be learned and experienced. I feel gates opening in so many areas. Yes, you absorb and you accept things as you go through life and if you are a Christian then you are constantly saying thank you. You must be ready to receive.

Some of my most precious moments have been well documented − my trip to Bangladesh for Tear Fund perhaps is the best known. That did stop me in my tracks. It was in a Bihari refugee camp where everyone, even the babies, had scabs and sores. I bent down near one of the children. At that moment a photographer wanted to take a picture and in the rush someone stood on the fingers of a child and there was a loud scream. I grabbed hold of him and forgot all about his dirt and sores. I remember his warm little body clinging to me and then his crying stopping. I realised there and then that I had an enormous amount to learn about practical Christian loving.

That moment almost drove me to giving up my career, all rather illogical since I am not qualified in medical matters. I thought what I was doing in the pop scene was a little easy, but I realised I was being stupid when one of the nurses pointed out to me that they needed me to tell people what was happening and I could aid by raising money. That's something I have tried to do.

EDWIN ROBERTSON

Edwin Robertson continues to exercise a powerful church ministry even though he is in his seventies. He is minister of Heath Street Baptist Church, Hampstead, London. He is a former Assistant Head of BBC Religious Broadcasting and has been a member of countless committees worldwide. He has written many books and is an authority on Bonhoeffer and William Barclay, on both of whom he has written critically acclaimed commentaries.

I've always been aware of God's presence. To me, life is a continual listening. I can remember chatting away with God when I was six or seven years old! I didn't have a name for God, then. I suppose my mother had talked to me about 'the heavenly Father' and I went to church.

In those younger days I was taken to an Irvingite church, of Catholic Apostolic tradition, and founded on the belief that it would close if Christ didn't come back.

I had a dated conversion. I was seventeen and I went to a meeting at the West Ham Central Mission (the Barking Road Tabernacle as it was called then). There was a campaign of sorts with a singing evangelist.

As I said, I had simply known there was a God with whom I was friendly and to whom I was committed. There was not a great deal of Jesus there. I had a tremendous sense that it was God who forgave me, a powerful sureness of being claimed by Him. Well, I got out of my seat — as they say — and claimed what the preacher said about God and Jesus.

Then I was baptised properly, a tremendous

experience. Once I had been a very private person with my beliefs; then came the decision to stand up at the evangelist's invitation, and now came baptism, out there in front of everyone.

Much was to come in my life: joys and sorrows, successes and disappointments. At one time I had designs on becoming a missionary but the Missionary Society ratted on me and I ended up with a scholarship to a theological college in Oxford!

And I'm still aware that His presence is always there with me.

DAVID SELF

David Self is the TV reviewer for **The Times Educational Supplement**. *He has compiled and broadcast countless programmes for radio and television and has been greatly involved with school broadcasting. He has compiled and written a number of books.*

There's a path I walk home along most nights.

On frosty winter evenings, away from the lights of cars and houses, I sometimes stop halfway to look up at the slowly wheeling constellations as they make their imperceptible annual progress across the sky.

Along that same path on summer evenings, especially after rain, the scents of stocks, carnations and a flower whose name I do not know linger magically in the air.

And it's in those moments, miraculously repeated many times a year, that I *know* that creation is more than chaotic chance. Between the infinite, mathematical precision of the heavens and the subtlety of those transient petals I *know* the truth of these words of Cardinal Newman:

> God has created me to do Him some definite purpose. He has committed some work to me which He has not committed to another. I have my mission. I may never know it in this world, but I shall be told it in the next.
>
> I am a link in the chain, a bond of connection between persons. He has not created me for naught . . . He knows what He is about . . . He may make

me feel desolate, make my spirits sink, hide my future from me . . . Still, He knows what He is about.

JOE SMITH

Joe Smith was a fisherman for forty-three years, from the age of fourteen until he was forced to retire with angina. He has been very much part of the Methodist witness in Buckie, Scotland, and the yearly Buckie Keswick that draws thousands of people.

It was a Friday, in January 1956. Most fishing boats had gone home because of a bad weather forecast and we were among the last. We were about twenty-five miles from Buckie when we received a distress call from another boat, the wooden-hulled, 65 feet in length, *Katreen*. Her engines had failed and they required assistance since they were drifting helplessly and the wind was blowing them towards land.

Our skipper answered the call and after locating the *Katreen* we secured a towline and started towing her at three thirty p.m. Our boat the *Briarbark* was 71 feet in length, steel-hulled and fairly powerful. It all seemed a straightforward affair.

But after an hour the towline snapped and once again the *Katreen* was being driven towards the rocks, as the wind had increased from the north-west (an onshore wind) to gale force. It was with much difficulty that we secured the towline again. This was to happen twice more and it was ten forty-five p.m. before we reached the harbour entrance.

The weather was really bad now and the conditions were atrocious, with heavy gusts accompanied by showers. To make matters worse the lights on the shore failed just at that particular moment. The backwash from the harbour wall was making it very difficult to control the boat on tow and as we were about to enter the safety of the channel our steering chains broke and we were soon out of control and being dashed against the outside of the harbour wall, near to some dangerous reefs. The other boat crashed down on top of our stern, severely damaging the wooden-hulled boat which the swell had drawn helplessly behind the breakwater near more rocks.

We were truly in the hands of God for our survival. It was impossible to survive in that area and disaster seemed imminent for both crews. The cook was a Christian and the two of us prayed that we would be delivered, for the sake of all the wives and families involved. There were thirteen men on the two boats. At the same time we cut the towline to the *Katreen* so that our boat could use the propeller. The towline was near the propeller and if it had fouled the blades we would have been unable to manoeuvre ahead or astern. During this time huge waves were breaking over both boats and it was difficult to see where we were without lights.

Just as it looked as if the *Katreen* and her crew were heading for disaster on the rocks, the sea became calm for two to three minutes. We were suddenly right alongside and the crew stepped on to our boat almost in dry feet! Amid the storm and turbulence God still calms seas. With the help of the two crews we were able amid atrocious conditions to carry out temporary repairs to our steering gear.

Somehow by divine guidance our skipper steered clear of the dangerous reefs behind Buckie harbour, even though the harbour lights were out of action. We went out into the Moray Firth till daylight and then came into the harbour. The quays were lined with thousands of people, thankful to see both crews safe.

All that remained of the *Katreen* were some splinters of planks that were washed over the pier. What a deliverance!

I hope someone may learn from this that God still calms the storms in our everyday lives, and that He is near us always, if we believe.

JOHN SMITH

❧

*John Smith has captured considerable media attention for his Christian work among the outlaw bike gangs and Hell's Angels in his home territory of Melbourne, Australia. He has become one of the most popular speakers at the British Greenbelt Festival and his book, **On The Side Of The Angels** (Lion), has met with wide acclaim.*

In 1972 John Smith and his wife Glena attended an Australian rock festival. What they found both surprised and offered a challenge.

We got into hundreds of conversations about Christianity during the weekend, many of them open and searching . . . There was a river running through the Sunbury site and once again there were people who wanted to be baptised. They felt that this was the place where they could best serve notice to their contemporaries that a change had taken place in their lives.

I didn't do the baptising myself this time, but I was in the thick of things and spoke to the crowd. It was a remarkable scene. These people were standing up to their knees in the muddy, slow-moving river, while naked and semi-naked people who had earlier been skinny-dipping, lounged around on the banks and made off-the-cuff remarks at us all.

One of those being baptised was a guy who had been part of an outlaw biker group. He had been a hard-drinking, hard-fighting reprobate, but had been personally transformed through his encounter with Jesus Christ. After he had been pulled out of the water,

113

he stood in mid-stream and told, in a simple and direct way, exactly what the gospel of Jesus meant. The audience was silenced by his sincerity and passion. And by the fact that he didn't use religious words, but language they understood. This was real communication.

For Glena, this was her first proper introduction to what had, for the last year or so, been my world. On the one hand she was shocked at the amount of drink and drugs consumed and by the completely casual attitude towards sex. But on the other hand she warmed immediately to the honesty of these people. She spent hours in conversation with different groups and individuals. She was struck, too, by the sheer number of kids who had only the vaguest sense of direction in their lives and no real belief or framework to live by. She sat on the side of the hill reading her Bible and came across some words of the prophet Joel which seemed to sum up everything we had experienced that weekend.

Tears streaming down her face, she showed me what she had been reading. It said, 'Multitudes, multitudes in the valley of decision'.

She looked across this sea of people and said, 'John, here they are. But where is the Church?' Glena, by her own route, had come to the same conclusions as me. We both understood why we were there. Because the Church plainly wasn't. True, the good old Salvation Army were dispensing free cool drinks with their customary gift of showing love in a practical way. And John Uren and Kevin Smith were there with a group helping them. But that was it. The Christian representation among this vast crowd was minimal. Glena and I both knew we were in the right place.

ADRIAN SNELL

From a very early age Adrian Snell exhibited exceptional musical talent and the furtherance of this, allied to his deeply felt Christian convictions, have meant a series of much acclaimed albums, live performances and special presentation of several musicals. A most congenial and friendly person, Adrian Snell has been one of the major pioneers within the Christian community to translate basic Christian truths into a manner and style that will communicate to the non-Christian. He lives in Leeds, is married and has several children.

At the age of only twenty-three, Adrian Snell already had three well received albums behind him. One of them, *Goodbye October*, was voted best British gospel album of 1976 by the British magazine *Buzz*

Born in Northwood, Middlesex, in 1954, educated at St Edmunds School, Canterbury and Leeds College of Music, and a Licentiate of the Guildhall School of Music, London, Adrian Snell is a multi-instrumentalist, composer and vocalist. He started playing the piano at the age of six, and by fifteen was integrating words and music in a very individualistic way. His music arrived at a time when the Christian world was looking for fairly contemporary material that would interest the secular music world and at the same time be appreciated by young Christians.

But, of course, much has happened since those early productive years and even if he has some years to come before he reaches his fortieth birthday there are those who see him as a veteran in the 'Jesus Music' world. His faith remains strong, and so too has been his commitment to music and word. For Adrian the best safeguard for the artist in his own somewhat shambolic world lies in a personal realtionship with God. He says, 'Whatever kind of musical star he may be, an artist is not a *spiritual* superstar'.

Through his career he has been aware that there are two problems facing a committed Christian who has worked in and around the sceptical rock industry: one is the fight for public acceptance of his work and the other is to overcome the apparent British reserve and mistrust of those who choose to be open about their faith.

His spiritual experience has been varied and he maintains that he has always been conscious of life being one total precious moment. His parents have been very influential. 'I count it as a real privilege to have had parents who were deeply committed Christians. It was *the* priority above everything in their lives. I have often heard them saying that from the time I and my brother and sister were born, they prayed for us every day that we would grow up to be Christians who were using what we had for God.'

And so, when speaking of, say, a conversion experience, a moment which many of us have experienced, he says, 'I believe that I've always had a meaningful relationship with God. Where I have grown is that I have come to understand that relationship more deeply.'

He speaks of experiences that have confronted him, causing him to reconsider future intentions. 'We say, ''Don't get committed. We are our own lords and masters.'' Then we sing ''Jesus Is Lord'' – and don't mean it most of the time. It makes me angry and at one time that was my condition. I've learned a lot about discipleship and the cost of commitment to Christ and responsibilities.'

His faith and conviciton remain strong and delight thousands worldwide.

JUDITH STEVENSON

~

Judith Stevenson has been a pioneer of dance in Christian worship. She has taken her God-given gifts worldwide and works closely with her husband Geoffrey, an extremely talented mime artist. Their work together is well described in the book **Steps of Faith** *(Kingsway).*

The church I attended in London as a young Christian was strongly evangelical, with good sound teaching, but the worship that was encouraged was very private and very personal. In other words, it wouldn't matter if there was no one else in the church, as long as there was me and my God. In complete contrast, when I moved to York I saw and heard prophecy and speaking in tongues and I even saw people raise their hands in a church service and smile! I hated it all. I was frightened of such emotionalism. I objected to seeing other people showing off their spirituality with such freedom and wondered indignantly how anyone could dare to presume a knowledge of God's mind by actually speaking his word in prophecy to the whole congregation!

Then I changed. When, how or why I don't know. But I had a growing and unmistakable awareness of being filled with the Holy Spirit. As this happened I knew God was calling on me to repent. To repent of my resentment and my judgmental attitudes toward others, and to repent of being self-centred. He asked me if I really loved him with all of my heart and soul and mind. He gave me a new love for himself. He also gave me a new love for my fellow Christians. Suddenly the most beautiful sight in the world for me was to see someone else caught up in adoration and worship of God. No matter how I felt, the fact that God was being worshipped and enjoyed by someone else was thrilling.

DONNA SUMMER

Donna Summer blazed a spectacular trail across the pop world towards the end of the seventies with one chart hit after another. It was early in 1976 that her record 'Love To Love You, Baby' became an international hit . . . and a scandal at the same time, as its lyrics and vocal quirks were criticised for being overtly erotic. Brought up in a Christian home and a believer when a teenager, Donna Summer re-found her faith. The hits have continued but the message has changed. Her passionate, bravura voice continues both to rivet and charm. Now very much a major star, Donna affirms life, love, womanhood and self. She won a Grammy nomination for the Best Inspirational Song category with her 'I Believe In Jesus'.

When I was a kid you had to compete. I was one of seven and to be heard you had to talk loud. Either that or you just tried to find an empty corner where you could sit and fantasise about being some place else. School wasn't any easier. I went to school with some pretty violent people, and I was an outsider because I couldn't live on that black-and-white separatist premise.

I went to church as a kid and I learned of God, Jesus and the power of the gospel to bring new life. I caught something of personal miracles and heard testimonies. I heard some of the great gospel singers.

I found myself very much in the music and show-biz world and I won a part in the musical *Hair*. In Munich I met the producer Giorgio Moroder. I made some recordings and eventually there was a hit record with 'Love To Love You, Baby'. It was a huge hit but it gained me, as with some subsequent hits, a sexy image. I think it was *Rolling Stone* that called me a servile vixen with a whispering voice.

My most precious moment was suddenly finding my way back to the faith I had known and yet never been totally committed to. I was to realise I had been part of some rather appalling things and I knew well that the devil tries to draw away people focusing on God. Fortunately I found friends, pop stars who were Christians and an understanding minister friend. I felt the weight of my past lifted and the anger and oppression of a diseased spirit taken away.

I still sing of love, but I also know God's love. Many of my songs are strong testimonies to the supernatural love of God.

RIGHT REVEREND HASSAN BARNABA
DEHQUNI-TAFTI

~

The Right Reverend Hassan Barnaba Dehquni-Tafti, Bishop in Iran and Bishop of the Episcopal Church in Jerusalem and the Middle East, told the following narrative in his sermon at the Missionary Service of the Virginia Theological College, Virginia, USA.

I relate to you the simple story of a person who travelled six hundred years within sixty years, who from his Muslim background came to know Christ through wrestlings within his soul which wounded him, shook him to the roots of his being, yet gave him joy and satisfaction and ultimate victory over unspeakable tragedy. His mother had become a Christian through the work of a missionary hospital in her home town in a Muslim country. She died when the boy was only four. In accordance with her will, a missionary friend of hers took the boy away from his village with the reluctant consent of his Muslim father, and put him in a missionary boarding school.

The boy grew up in a world of tension – the tension between his Muslim family background and the foreign missionary atmosphere, the tension between his own national and ethnic cultural background and the seeming foreign atmosphere of the Church. Having lived through all these tensions, he finally decided, when he was young, to give himself to Christ and to serve His Church. From childhood he felt like Isaiah, 'Before I was born, the Lord appointed me; he made me his servant' (Isaiah 49.3).

The boy decided to serve his Lord and his Church

in his own country. It was a Church born with great travail out of a century of missionary work in the traditional missionary way of which he himself was one of the fruits. The Church needed indigenous ministry very badly. In his own country's university he became exposed to new tensions. In the years during and after the Second World War Communism was fashionable among the students in Iran. Our young man had to go through it all. In the University of Teheran in those days the Communist manifesto was much more read and revered than the Sermon on the Mount or, indeed, the Muslim Holy Writings. His faith was shaken, but never completely annihilated. In the end it became stronger than ever and he was ready to start his theological training. With no theological college in the country he was sent to England for training. There he had to experience fresh and fearful tensions. The rapid social changes that he had to go through nearly crushed him. The tension between the two cultures upset him more than at any other time in his life. Who was he? Where did he belong? Who were his people? Through the friendship of a wise man of God who understood him, his faith was restored. He came to know the simple meaning of faith, which was trusting the God of love, no matter what happened. He belonged to Christ and he was a member of the Body of Christ, whose members are always strangers in this world and citizens of the heavenly country, no matter to which country they belong.

When he had finished his studies he went back to his own country and to his own Church with a new vision and a deeper, quieter faith. Later on he was happily married to a Christian girl who shared his vision of building up the Church in their country. As he grew in faith he was given more and more responsibility, until when he was middle-aged he became the most responsible person in his Church.

The testing time of his life came during the Iranian Revolution. The tiny Church he was serving came under severe attack. Some church members left the country. He was advised to leave also, or give in to the illegal groups of fanatics who came and took the Church's buildings, but he was led by God to stand up to the unlawful acts and to the injustices. He, like some others, suffered severely as a result. During the first week of the revolution one of the pastors of the Church was brutally murdered. Building after building belonging to the Church was taken over. His home and offices were attacked and looted. Early one morning assassins came to his bedroom and fired five shots at his head. His wife, who threw herself across him, was wounded, but he was miraculously saved. Six months later when he was in Cyprus on church duty news reached him that assassins had shot and killed his only son, an Oxford graduate with an MA from George Washington University, who had gone back to do his national service.

The question is, was it all worth it? Was the missionary activity for over a century in Iran all a mistake? Should he have never become a Christian? Would it be right for him to cry, like Jeremiah, and say, 'O Lord, thou hast deceived me, and I was deceived.'

The man is no other than the one who is speaking to you now.

And the answer, as far as I'm concerned, is that despite the difficulties involved – psychological, sociological and cultural – it has all been worth it.

CECILY TAYLOR

Cecily Taylor is a poet and lyricist; her main collection of poems is entitled **Contact**. *Formerly a teacher, for many years she has been involved in community relations.*

I had walked through a wild meadow, buttercups gold-dusting my shoes, and reached the mown slopes of a park stretching down to a lake. As I neared the water I could see a family of ducklings with their attentive mother – half a dozen bells of fluff-feathers surprised at the new wet world they were able to move across, so light that gravity was the last thing on their minds. I sat on a nearby bench while spring sunshine lit the scene, somehow especially golden as only light on brand new leaves can be, before summer paints them a darker green.

Placed within time it was May 1980, an oasis of a day within a chunk of years in which tranquillity was an extremely rare commodity. But the park with the ducklings was brimming over with it, and an incredible peace wrapped me round, permeating my being so that nothing else mattered, because I too had become part of it. There was a feeling of being linked with something vast, for its very essence seemed to fill everything.

My concept of time – past, present and future – was like an enormously long narrow carpet. Looking back I couldn't see where it began; there was the present piece I was standing on and all of the future was already there too, but rolled up in front of me – ready to unwind slowly.

The overwhelming understanding within me was

that if I stopped struggling in my own strength and plugged into this goodness and love in an act of trust, then I truly needn't worry about anything ever again – just like those ducklings, never concerned that the water might not support them.

After a long while I got out a notebook, as poets are inclined to do where other people reach for cameras, and started to jot down words to try and encapsulate my impression; an impossible task of course because it belonged to a wordless dimension.

By the time I left the park a kind of poem had evolved, and this is probably as near as I am ever likely to get in defining what I called this 'Spirit of Affirmation':

I am the way that stretches out before –
I am the journey you are on,
I am the present moment that you tread –
I am the next place that you stand upon.

I am the air you breathe –
I am of every part and of the whole,
I am the love you cannot fall beyond –
I am the inner silence of your soul.

I am the question that you ask –
I am the answer that you crave,
I am the reality of truth,
I am the ever-living thread that leaps the grave.

I am all time in now,
I am this minute to begin,
I am the one that you have always known;
I am the peace that you may dwell within.

ROY TREVIVIAN

~

Roy Trevivian was ordained as a Methodist minister, serving churches on the Liverpool Docks and in the Old Kent Road, London. Eight years later he was ordained an Anglican priest. After parish work he became a full-time radio producer with the BBC. He became a distinguished broadcadster and, as a producer, was responsible for the very popular programme **Speak Easy** *that was presented by Jimmy Savile and broadcast on the BBC's pop channel, Radio 1. Roy also was instrumental in bringing Paul Simon to public notice when Paul, then virtually unknown, was living in Britain.*

It was 1969. I was working with the BBC and they asked me to go to Jerusalem and with a tape recorder describe my thoughts and feelings at all the holy places.

It was a Thursday night (which I didn't realise at the time). It was ten p.m. I was sitting in my hotel room listening to the recordings that I had made that day. For no rational reason I decided to go to the Garden of Gethsemane there and then. (It was on a Thursday night that Jesus went there for the last time, but I wasn't thinking about that at the time.) I left the room and as I was walking out of the hotel the manager asked me where I was going. I told him. 'You won't get in at this time of night, but if you wait till the morning I will arrange for you to get in. They lock the gate at night,' he said. I thanked him and left the hotel.

Gethsemane wasn't far away. Before I got there I had the idea of climbing over the wall if the gate was indeed locked. Not a hope – the walls around the garden were much too high to climb over. I arrived at the gate, to find it very securely locked. I carried on walking round the wall. Eventually I had to walk up a dark track in order to continue following the wall. I was frightened. There could easily have been a terrorist or a 'mugger' hiding in the dark, waiting for some idiot like me. Then I came to the spot where the wall was being rebuilt. The workmen had knocked down a part of the wall and all I had to do was clamber over.

I remember feeling like a thief. I had no right to go into that garden without permission, and I am not by nature a law-breaker. Nevertheless, I went in. In the dark the garden looked small. There didn't seem to be any grass, but there were some trees, olive trees I supposed (after all, it was on the Mount of Olives). I tried to imagine where Jesus would have knelt that night he struggled with his Father to avoid the crucifixion.

I chose a spot right opposite where the gate in the wall of Jerusalem would have been when Jesus entered the city in triumph and I sat down on the soil. Jerusalem looked breathtakingly beautiful. The dome of the Mosque there was floodlit and the gold of the dome shone brightly. Cars drove past on the road outside the garden.

I began to think about Jesus. What was going on in his mind all those years ago when he had been in that garden on that night? And then he came! I wasn't being deluded. I know the difference between thinking about someone and actually being confronted by them. They are completely different experiences. He was there.

'What then,' I asked, 'was your struggle in this

garden all about?' He told me, 'It was about being true to myself.' He said, 'A lot of me wanted to run away from what was going to happen.' I just can't speak about the rest. It is all there inside me but for reasons that I can't understand, I mustn't touch with my thoughts the full content of what happened.

What I can say is that he accepted who he was. That he chose to be himself. He was the Saviour. It was in his power to offer the salvation of freddom to every human being and no matter what the cost he was going to offer it. And that is exactly what he did.

And me? What did that encounter do for me? I left the garden that night knowing that there was only one way for me to go and that was to follow my own integrity, to be true to the self that God had created me to be.

I haven't succeeded. I have failed a thousand times. I have sought praise and acted to get it, I have been false for fear of being rejected, I have sinned and kept it secret, I have pretended to love when I haven't felt loving.

I know, though, where life is; I know the pathway to the truth. I know that human life can have eternal significance. I know that every human being is of infinite worth. I know that within this vast universe there is the love of a God who is personal, that the meaning of the whole of creation is about love. I don't believe these things to be true, I know that they are.

I have only travelled a very short distance along the road. It is up to others, more courageous and loving than I am, to go further.

Finally, though, I have to admit that when I say I know there is God and that God is love, it isn't knowledge in the sense that I can communicate it.

It isn't objective knowledge. It cannot be
demonstrated. I have experienced three times a vivid
sense of the presence of Jesus. I believe that they
were genuine experiences.

Lord I believe that you are there
Forgive me when the darkness comes
and my faith begins to waver.

SHEILA WALSH

*Sheila Walsh is one of the foremost British artists involved in the 'Jesus Music' and white gospel field. She has recorded numerous albums, tasted briefly general chart fortune with her song 'Drifting' and hosted several series of the **Rock Gospel** show on television. Much given to touring, her work has been heard and appreciated worldwide. She is married to Norman Miller and now lives in the United States where she has recorded, played 'live' performances and hosted a television show with evangelist Pat Robertson.*

One particular day at London Bible College changed my future. Each term we had a quiet day, with no regular lectures. We had a morning and evening chapel service and the rest of the time was spent alone with the Lord. The speaker at morning chapel had chosen as his text Isaiah 43.18–21. The verse that jumped out at me was verse 18: 'Remember not former things, nor think on the things of old; behold, I do a new thing. Now it springs forth. Do you not perceive it?'

After chapel I went off to the woods near our college with my Bible and my daily notes. I turned to the assigned passage for that day, to find it was Isaiah 43.18. Later that day I was back in my room, lying on my bed, thinking about the verse, when a friend of mine popped in to see me. She was a very gifted artist and had copied, in her exquisite copper-plate handwriting, the theme verse for our quiet day, as a gift – Isaiah 43.18. I knew that God was trying to say something to me, but I had no idea what. As far as I was concerned, my past was a closed book, with no bearing on my future.

I went down at ten o'clock to watch the news in the student common room and suddenly became embarrassingly aware that I was about to burst into tears. I rushed upstairs and fell on my bed, and wept and wept. I felt as if I was groaning deep inside myself, but the cause of my grief was a mystery to me. Feeling I needed help, I knocked on the door of one of my friends at about midnight. I told her of my confusion and she suggested that we got down on our knees and asked God to speak. After some time she said to me that she didn't know too much about my family, but felt that God was trying to tell me something about my father. I knew that she was right.

As I began to allow God gently to open a long-closed door, I felt able for the first time to face the reality of a hurt that had coloured my life. I realised that in all my years as a Christian I had never prayed to God as Father. I guess that seemed to me to be a negative image of God. I went back to my room and all that night I sat on my bed, with my *Cruden's Concordance* and my Bible, looking up all the references to Father and rejoicing in them. I went to Mr Kirby the next day and asked leave to go home to Scotland for a few days.

My mum and I shed many tears together that weekend, as she answered questions concerning my dad that I'd never been able to pose before, but the tears felt good. As I looked through our photograph albums, at pictures of us all, I was grateful that I had had a father who loved me and had now found peace with the Lord.

ROSEMARY WASS

～

Rosemary Wass is a farmer in West Yorkshire and a Methodist lay preacher. She is President of the British Methodist Church's women's group, Network. From September 1990 she assumes the post of Vice-President in the Methodist Church, this being the highest honour that can come to a lay person in that Church.

It has been a strange day. The morning had dawned after a good night's sleep but it would have been good to have been able to sleep on – I was still tired. Breakfast and the chores of the day had to be dealt with and things progressed steadily. The afternoon came and a chance to shell peas and watch the opening game of Wimbledon . . . and still I was tired. The afternoon wore on and my uneasiness grew. A call to the doctor, a blue flashing ambulance and crisp white cotton sheets. Queries and questions and yet a fantastic peace of heart and mind. 'This is beyond me,' I thought. 'It doesn't matter any more. I'm in God's hands.' Injections and intermittent sleep and emergency surgery and a long sleep.

I awoke and knew that whatever had had to be done was done and now I was on the way to recovery and home (always the goal). Gradual progression towards walking and eating and the doctor at the end of the bed, promising me new pastures – the 'half-way' house between surgery and home. Fresh air – a ride in an ambulance and a new bed and fellow patients. I was disappointed not to be able to go home – I wanted my family – away from hospital routine and discipline. My hair needed washing and my toenails trimming. I needed a bit of extra attention! But no, I was in a ward with elderly long-stay patients who needed their limbs rubbing and their hearing aids tuning. I didn't feel at home; I didn't belong.

Visiting time came and went and I was alone in a 'Mount Everest' of a bed. My hopes had been dashed – I was not as well as I thought.

My bed was hard and unyielding with a new mattress that might just as well have been a board. I lay unhappy with my immediate prospects, listening to the moans and sighs of those with less future ahead of them than me. My mind was filled with the same recurring theme: 'Together'; 'I am with you!'; 'We are together'; 'Together in Christ'. And I knew again the peace that I had known at the outset. And the knowledge of not being alone never left me, and gave me a gift way beyond myself to do what I could and make those elderly women's lives more bearable, and helped me to cope with long nights.

When I did go home, there was great rejoicing – but times of great frustration too. I had to learn to be gracious in receiving love and help and knowing that my recuperation was a time to enjoy the company of others as they visited. I look back on my indisposition as a privilege because of the way God filled my life through it!

On 19th April, 1988, I was in New York City, teeming with traffic, packed with people, stacked with buildings. Early evening gave opportunity for some sightseeing – so I visited the Empire State Building. No longer the highest building in the city, but nevertheless, there is a fantastic panorama of the River Hudson from the top. I looked down on a suddenly miniature view of roads and vehicles and a jungle of concrete. Dusk was coming. The lights of church spires and big businesses came on here and there – I was seeing New York City in a new perspective.

The evening light was changing and a dusky pink fringed the horizon all round. Every now and then a plane weaved its way across the darkening dome, and as daylight gracefully gave way to night a kind of fairyland grew below, and above in the great blue sky the stars began to sparkle and the moon shone out.

This was the night that history was to be made – when Venus would be in a special relationship to the moon, a scene which nature could not repeat for thousands of years. And so I waited – and there it was! Easily visible and quite beautiful – Venus lay at the tip of the moon. Not man-made, but God-made. And it was good. I was speechless. I looked at man's creation of concrete and lifted my head high to worship the God of nature. And it was very good!

PAULINE WEBB

Pauline Webb is one of the best known women in mainstream denominational Christianity. She has been a member of numerous world-based groups and committees, and was both the youngest occupant of the British Methodist Churches post of General Secretary of the Overseas Division and also the elected Vice President. In recent time she has been the head of religious programmes for the BBC's World Service. Now retired, she is in much demand as a speaker and preacher.

People with half-faces usually wear masks. Salvation is the discovery in life as well as in death of that essential me that lies behind the mask, the restoration of that whole face that has been so marred, even in the hands of the sculptor.

Sometimes one does meet a 'saved' person who bears about herself a quality of being wholly alive, totally aware of her own identity and conscious of her own worth. Such assurance arises from the experience of loving and being loved. Some women paradoxically become most sure of their identity when in fact they lose it in the life of another, taking on in marriage another's name and life-style and finding the meaning of their own lives through sharing the lives of husbands and children. Yet even within that identification there remains the need for a sense of personal identity, for a 'room of one's own', as Virginia Woolf put it, in which one is aware of one's individual worth. I treasure especially the memory of one beautiful though deserted woman I met in a village in India, whose dignity and sense of personal worth made an indelible impression upon me. She had neither husband nor child with whom to identify. In the eyes of many she would have seemed a pitiable person. She lived in a poverty-stricken community where her husband left her because she was childless. She eked out a starvation-level existence on a wage of 10p a day. She was illiterate, though very articulate. She told me in good evangelical language which I have never forgotten, 'Jesus Christ didn't only save me, he made me realise that my life was worth saving.'

What was Deena's life worth? To many she still seemed to be an 'outcaste', the old name for the community to which she belonged. To some she was now known by the prouder name of harijan, a child of God, as Mahatma Gandhi had insisted on calling the poorest of India's people. To a Christian doctor who had saved Deena's life by giving an emergency transfusion of her own blood when Deena had been desperately ill, she was a patient worth giving skill and blood to save. And to Deena herself, the full worth of life was expressed in the words and acts of a Christian presbyter and a common cup of wine, with the declaration of Jesus to us both: 'This is my body which is broken for you. This is my blood which is shed for you.' We were both of the same value, bought with the same price, forgiven by the same love, given a unique worth. It was in that gospel that Deena, living as she was in all the deprivation of Asia, and I, sated with the affluence of the West, both found our essential identity.

MARY WHITEHOUSE

Since she founded the National Viewers and Listeners Association Mary Whitehouse has become a household name in her fight for better standards in broadcasting.

I've been seen as a frosty old fuddy-duddy with winged spectacles and a blue rinse. I've never been that kind of person. I found that very hard, but what has been extraordinary has been the way the Lord has used it. I think half my audience come genuinely because they want to hear me and the other half come and see what this crazy woman really looks like.

I long ago came to accept that if the Lord wanted me to do this work, whatever happened was in his hands and not mine. So I really felt quite at peace about it. In the summer of 1963 I was an art teacher in Shropshire. I wrote to the Director General of the BBC, concerned by what I saw as the falling standards of broadcasting. It was the time of the 'swinging sixties' and television programmes were getting increasingly permissive, with increased sex, violence and bad language. I was appalled by what I saw.

My distress came not from the moral indignation of an out-of-touch prig, but real distress from what I saw around me. As a senior school mistress I had to deal with five different incidents, including a serious sexual one, and each stemmed back to something seen or heard on television.

I had support from friends and we launched a petition. I rang the Birmingham *Evening Mail* and a reporter came to interview me and asked if we were going to hold our proposed meeting in the Birmingham

Town Hall. I said yes. I didn't realise it held 2,000. But the nationals picked up on the story and within a few days letters poured in. We made 40,000 signatures our target and we received half a million. It was the start of what was to become the National Viewers and Listeners Association.

I said at that first meeting that if violence is constantly portrayed as normal on the television screen you will help to create a violent society. I didn't think it was a very profound statement, it just seemed common sense.

I was in my early fifties when all this began and I'm now seventy-eight. Time flies! I think the crisis moment, the moment of truth for me, that would sow the seed for what I would do eventually, came when at the age of twenty I fell in love with a married man. I went to a meeting in Wolverhampton held by the Oxford Group. They preached on four absolute standards: absolute honesty, absolute purity, absolute unselfishness and absolute love.

I really felt this was what I wanted to do and I gave my life to God at this point and asked him to lead and direct me. It was the important turning point. And at that same meeting I met Ernest. We became part of the same preaching team and married in January 1940.

I have had my vision that has kept me going through hard times. I recall once I was walking up Fleet Street in London at a time of very great stress and I remember it as a sort of light, and the Lord said to me, 'Mary, if you continue to carry the burden yourself, it will kill you. Give it to me and I will carry it for you!'

I think when the history of this century comes to be written, it will show that we allowed those with access to television, in particular, to undermine our values, our standards and our beliefs and we were so afraid of getting involved that many of us just buried ourselves in our personal affairs and hoped that our families would not be affected by the changing moral climate. Alas, not all these hopes were realised. But, thank God, many young people today are realising there is a better way.

STELLA WISEMAN

◞

Stella Wiseman is in her early twenties and graduated in English from Nottingham University. She has worked as an editor with Tear Fund and more recently with **Where** *magazine.*

I went off Christmas several years ago – probably around the time I started combining festive preparations with a job. Too much hassle to greet the Christ Child who's been submerged in his manger of tinsel while the Three Wise Men get drunk at the office party. Add to that the tension and you have a poor recipe for celebration.

The tension – it builds up on Sunday evening, till my stomach is alternately a tight knot and a turbulent sea. My sleep is no less turbulent as I become increasingly angry, but at what or whom I don't know. The immediate problem is work, combined with overcrowded public transport and its inability to run on time. The long term problem is of course me and my inability to stop worrying. All of which keeps me very slim. The tension lessens as the week draws on – it's purely a psychological end-of-weekend syndrome. Or at least it *was* (O ye of little faith: This is in the past now) up until last Christmas.

It was a particularly bad Sunday. I'd stayed in bed till noon feeling groggy and depressed, which is always a poor way of starting the day, but very easy to do if you've no particular plans. The sleepless night followed right on cue, as did the anger, the tension and the self-pity (didn't I mention that before?). I did pray, but with the knowledge that there was something I had to do. There was no obvious excuse for staying at home, so by the time I crawled to my desk I was muttering oaths worthy of Macbeth's witches. No fit mood for a Carol Service in the evening, but promises are promises and though I was deliberately late (well, it *was* a long walk) I duly sorted carol sheets and directed choir members to the loo with as much or as little grace as I could muster. Which perhaps made me vulnerable to the simplicity of it all – that Christ was born to make a difference to misery, depression, anger, tension, guilt, self-pity. To those feelings which start small and build up until they are larger than life, drawing you in on yourself and threatening not only your enjoyment of life, but your self-confidence, your work, your relationships, your health or worse.

I think it was during 'The First Noel' that it happened. Most suitable really, since it all began then. We were singing happily and out of tune, and even I was beginning to enjoy myself. I had an agnostic boyfriend once who agreed to come to church when staying with my parents. 'Nothing like a good sing,' he commented, and he was right, though it had no obvious impact on his beliefs. Anyway, we were singing and quite simply it occurred to me that it was true. There *was* a baby born in Bethlehem some 2,000 years ago, and that baby made a difference, a difference to me as an individual. I wasn't sure how, but it put my tension in perspective. Something to do with God being on earth and caring what happened to me. It gave me courage and the determination to stop worrying and feeling sorry for myself. In fact I became quite angry about letting myself slip into such a state.

It's not much in the face of tens of thousands killed

146

by an earthquake, or dying for lack of food, or even in the face of a single bereavement, but it's something that makes me look beyond myself. Which is a start.

OPEN HEART, OPEN HANDS

John Glass

Much of our anxiety, stress and frustration in trying to live as Christians comes about because of closed areas in our lives. This book enables Christians, with the aid of the Holy Spirit, to examine every corner of their personalites for areas that can be opened up to God, and to learn to *receive* in order that they might give.

Pocket paperback 017740 160 pp

AIM FOR EXCELLENCE

Tom Walker

Aim for Excellence is Tom Walker's appeal to Christians not to acquiesce to secular materialism, but to set out to improve their own standards. Every area of Christian life can be worked upon to make it a valuable aspect of the new dynamic Christian witness.

Pocket paperback 016140 160 pp

RADIANT CHRISTIAN LIVING

Melvin Banks with David Lee

A thoroughly down-to-earth investigation into God's conditions for a radiant, blessed life. Firmly grounded in Scripture, and authenticated by the experiences of well-known Pentecostal healing evangelist, Melvin Banks. Amusing, faith-provoking and intensely practical.

Pocket paperback 015063 160 pp

THE GREATEST MIRACLE

Melvin Banks

Melvin Banks shows how the Bible is the 'book of miracles'. Each chapter then details ways in which the life of Christ is miraculous. His character, His claims, His cross, His resurrection, and His coming-again. The book concludes with a powerful chapter on the miracle of Christ's life in its wholeness, and its challenge today.

Pocket paperback   016469   128 pp

HEALING SECRETS

Melvin Banks

Melvin Banks recounts further stories of divine healing at work, but also takes a step back from the scene of his crowded meetings to attempt to answer some fundamental and difficult questions about faith and suffering.

Pocket paperback   013567   160 pp

POWER FOR LIVING

Melvin Banks

Power for Living has something to say to everyone! As Melvin Banks writes, 'There is no-one who cannot do more with their life than they are doing at the moment'. The author shows how to deal effectively with inferiority, fatigue, nervous stress and exhaustion, insomnia, anxiety and tension.

Writing for Christians and unbelievers alike, Melvin Banks points the way to living a Spirit-filled life centred on Jesus, and free from guilt and frustration. A warm, often humorous and sensitive book to inspire everyone to live life to the full.

Pocket paperback   01881X   196 pp